9.99

D1029830

THE
SPYMASTER'S
HANDBOOK

THE SPYMASTER'S HANDBOOK

Michael Kurland

Facts On File Publications
New York ● Oxford

THE SPYMASTER'S HANDBOOK

Copyright © 1988 by Michael Kurland

Grateful acknowledgment is paid to the following for permission to reprint material in this book:

Excerpt from *Foreign Intelligence: The Ethics of the Craft*, by Arthur L. Jacobs, pp. 14-21; © 1982 by Arthur L. Jacobs. Reprinted from *Freedom at Issue* (May-June, 1982) by permission of Freedom House.

Excerpt from *Inside the Aquarium*, by Viktor Suvorov, p. 131; © 1986 by Viktor Suvorov. Reprinted by permission of Macmillan Publishing Company, USA, and Hamisch Hamilton, Ltd., UK.

Excerpt from *A Drink to Yesterday*, by Manning Coles, p. 134; © 1967 by Manning Coles. Reprinted by permission of Curtis Brown, Ltd.

Drawing by Peter Arno, p. 132; © 1938, 1966 The New Yorker Magazine, Inc.

Four panels from *Positively Pogo*, by Walt Kelly, p. 146; © 1955 by Walt Kelly. Reprinted by permission of Walt Kelly Estate, Selby Kelly, Executor.

All rights reserved. No part of this book may be reproduced or utilized in any form or by any means, electronic or mechanical, including photocopying, recording, or by any information storage and retrieval systems, without permission in writing from the publisher.

Library of Congress Cataloging-in-Publication Data

Kurland, Michael.
    The spymaster's handbook.

    Bibliography: p.
    Includes index.
    1. Espionage—Anecdotes, facetiae, satire, etc.
I. Title.
UB270.K87   1988   327.1′2′0207   88-3577
ISBN 0-8160-1314-4

Designed by Ron Monteleone

Printed in the United States of America

10 9 8 7 6 5 4 3 2 1

ACKNOWLEDGMENT

I would like to thank Kate Kelly for invaluable assistance; her editorial judgment has improved the book, and her unfailing good humor has made it possible.

CONTENTS

Courtesy of the New York Public Library Collection

NTRODUCTION

*G*entlemen do not read other people's mail.

—*Henry L. Stimson*

This book is a potpourri of information on spies and spying. About nine parts fact to one part fiction[1], it is designed to give you a feeling for what it is like to be a player in the game of espionage. It will provide you with enough background so that when the newly-elected president of Freedonia says to you, "George,"—he knows you only as "George"—"I want *you* to head our new Secret Service," you will have some idea of how to proceed beyond merely designing the uniform.

To keep the distinction between fact and fiction as clear as possible, all the pieces that are fiction will be marked at their start with a hand.[2] The "facts" are stated clearly and a bibliography is included at the end of the book; you can judge for yourself. But in the murky world of spy and counterspy, it is often difficult to tell what is true from what someone wants

---

[1]   Fiction because it sometimes makes a point clearer and faster than fact. An MI.5 (British Counterintelligence) handbook written during WWII quotes Lord Peter Wimsey, and the CIA used to buy a copy of every fictional spy book published for its library at Langley, Virginia, until a cost-conscious director put an end to the practice.

[2]   Like this:

you to believe is true; and what is admittedly false is often more honest than what is purportedly true.

The depiction of the spy in fiction has vacillated from the romantic adventurism of Oppenheim, Le Queux, and Fleming, to the paranoid anti-heroism of Le Carré, and has made most of the stops in between. The real-life spy has covered at least as broad a spectrum; to anything that you can say about spies in general, you can find at least one important exception.

Courtesy of the New York Public Library Collection

The common informer.
I confess, it is my nature's plague
To spy into abuses; and off it, my jealousy
Shapes faults that are not.

— Othello

And the life of a spy is a study in inconsistency: The most important rule is that there are no rules. The most common expectation is surprise. The most successful agent is the one you never hear of.

The career of espionage is usually not a rewarding one. Spies have been praised, but mostly they have been reviled; they have been thanked, but mostly they have been ignored; they have been rewarded, but mostly they have been disowned. Napoleon, who used spies in warfare more effectively than any previous commander, said, "The spy is a natural traitor." Henry L. Stimson, when serving as President Hoover's secretary of state, closed down the U.S. Navy's "Black Chamber" codebreaking section with the statement, "Gentlemen do not read other people's mail."

The emperor and the secretary were both mistaken. The spy is often a natural patriot, acting from motives so pure and ideals so lofty that even his enemies admire him. Which does not stop those enemies from hanging him if they catch him. Examples of this noble breed include the American Nathan Hale, the British Major André, and the Russian Richard Sorge. And the Gentlemen and Ladies who run the governments of the world have long since decided that reading other people's mail is an acceptable way of making sure that their intentions are honorable.

In recent years the status of espionage has once again come under attack in many Western democracies, as pundits once again confuse an instrument of policy with the makers of that policy. Which is not to say that there are no natural limits to the use and the usefulness of espionage in a free society. Totalitarian governments use their secret police as an instrument of control over their own people—a practice that was invented thousands of years ago. This we cannot allow. It is better that a hundred spies go unpunished than that one innocent citizen is put in fear of his government.

The practice of the spy is evolving along with the techniques of espionage. We will look at where it has been, what it did while there, and try to figure out where it is going, and what signposts it should follow.

PART ONE:
THE RUDIMENTS

And Moses sent them to spy out the land of Canaan . . . and see the land, what it is; and the people that dwelleth therein, whether they be strong or weak, few or many.

—Numbers 13:17–18

Back at the beginnings of the human experience, it has been said, the three primordial professions emerged: the shaman, the harlot, and the spy. These soon subdivided—the shaman becoming priest, politician, and doctor; the prostitute going into the other performing arts; and the spy becoming detective, journalist, scholar, and ambassador.

Over the intervening centuries these three original occupations slid into disrepute and disfavor. The shaman is now generally thought of merely as a quack, or an amusing witch doctor in some primitive tribe. Prostitution, once practiced by specially honored priestesses in marble temples, is now a street crime. And spies are now pictured as cowardly creatures who sell out their own country's secrets for the money to buy flashy cars, or as suave thugs who have been well trained to kill, but not to think.

What we have here is largely a problem in semantics.

If Sir Andrew Aguecheek, director of His Majesty's arsenal at Ulwitch, takes 20 golden sovereigns for the secrets of England's new smoothbore muzzle-loading twenty-pounders, then Sir Andrew is a traitor, but he is not a spy. He took information that he already possessed and used it for his gain and to the detriment of his country.

Courtesy of CULVER PICTURES

The Lord said to Moses, "Send men to spy out the land of Canaan, which I give to the people of Israel; from each tribe of their fathers shall you send a man, every one a leader among them."

—Numbers 13, 1-3

If Bardolpho, while in the pay of a foreign power, sneaks into London to murder Sir John Falstaff, he is an assassin, not a spy.

But Sir Toby Belch—who assumed the identity of Don Tobaso Y Belchismo 20 years ago, and lived in King Philip's very castle gathering information on the Armada—now he may be a spy, but he's no traitor. Artfully he snuck into an enemy country, and thence into a secured place in that country, to gather information upon which may depend the survival of his native land.

Suppose you have been named spymaster general of a new intelligence agency, created to safeguard the interests of Freedonia. You have been entrusted with the job of establishing this new agency, the Freedonian Intelligence Bureau, or FIB, which has the mission of safeguarding all allied interests outside Freedonian territory.

In order to perform your duties, the rudiments of intelligence—the methods, meanings and morals—must be known to you, if they aren't already. . . .

WHAT IT'S ALL ABOUT

Sssh! This is spy stuff!

—Chicolini
from Duck Soup

METHODS AND MEANINGS

A few pages from now we'll make some attempt to discuss the ethics and morality of espionage, but before we go any further, just to be sure we're all talking about the same thing at the same time, let us define our terms. We'll go through some of the more important words pertaining to or used by the intelligence community, defining them as they are usually used within the secret services.[1]

Espionage is the act of gathering confidential information or conducting clandestine operations in one country or entity for the benefit of another. The definition is quite independent of one's moral view of the act, since we must assume that one tends to think that one's own spies are noble, self-sacrificing, unsung heroes, while the opposition's agents are diabolically clever fiends who delight in maiming small children. We would, however, exclude investigative reporting from this definition.[2]

---

[1] For a much more extensive, although more terse, listing, see the intelligence glossary on pp. 161-65.

[2] Unless, of course, it's being done in the United States by TASS.

5

According to our determination, the information being gathered must be confidential, which means that the act is, to some extent, country-specific; what is open information in one country may be of uttermost secrecy in another. In the United States, for example, financial, economic, technical, and even military[3] information is published by the government. And that which isn't is ferreted out by teams of eager reporters. In the Soviet Union, even the Moscow telephone book is classified information, unavailable to the comrade-in-the-street.

Intelligence is the raw information concerning others upon which governments or other entities base their decisions and actions. It may be **covert intelligence**, information the subject does not wish you to have that is gathered by espionage, or in another clandestine manner; or **overt intelligence**, that culled from public sources or other openly available information. Intelligence agencies, such as the CIA, gather both sorts for use in their plans and estimates. Usually an *intelligence* agency uses *espionage*, or the results of espionage, but be aware that the two words are not synonyms.

There are different sorts of intelligence, depending on the needs of the **consumer**—the person, agency, governmental branch, or service that is in need of the end product.

Military Intelligence is information gathered for the use of the Army, Navy, or Air Force. It can be **Tactical Intelligence**, which is of immediate use at a low level, such as just where those enemy tanks are out there; **Operational Intelligence**, which would tell corps or army commanders what the opposing generals are planning for the next few weeks or so; or **Strategic Intelligence**, which is of long-term utility at a higher level, such as, if the Third Reich invades Poland, will Great Britain and France really declare war? Much of it, but not all, is of a directly military nature: the order of battle[4] of the enemy or potential enemy,[5] the secret war plans, the capabilities of new weapons, the level of training of enemy troops, the stock of spare parts, the specific areas in which troops are being trained or the specific equipment with which they are being equipped.[6] But of equal importance are accurate maps of just about everywhere, up-to-the-minute knowledge of weather conditions,[7] information on food and fuel stocks, the general condition of railroad marshalling yards and rolling stock, the type of soil in the area,[8] the morale of the population and its confidence in the

---

[3]　A defector from the Polish Secret Service was asked how many agents they had checking on American Army troop movements. He shrugged. "None," he said. "We read *Stars and Stripes* [the U.S. Army newspaper]."

[4]　Order of battle: equals the current or planned number, condition, and disposition of troops, weapons, equipment, and supplies.

[5]　To the military everyone is a potential enemy. This may not be as paranoid as it sounds; making and keeping *friends* is in the hands of the politicians.

[6]　NATO intelligence has noted the care with which the "purely defensive" Soviet troops in Eastern Europe are trained at river crossing, and the Soviet tanks are equipped with

government, the stability of the country's money supply and its ability to borrow on the international market.

Above strategic intelligence is what is called **Policy Intelligence**, which deals with those aspects of foreign affairs that are left to politicians and government agencies.

Besides military intelligence, a country might indulge in **Diplomatic Intelligence**, **Political Intelligence**, **Economic Intelligence**, **Industrial Intelligence**, and any number of other forms. These are all mixtures of covert and overt, and are conducted at all levels, from tactical to policy.

As spymaster general of Freedonia, you follow the FIB's mandate, which, like that of the CIA, forbids it from activities at home. The FIB will have its own intelligence-gathering functions, besides being the central collection point for **product**[9] from the many other competing intelligence agencies in

Courtesy of CULVER PICTURES

Freedonian counterintelligence officers frisking a Sylvanian spy(?).

---

river-crossing air-breathers. Curiously, the major north-south rivers—the Loire, the Seine, the Rhine, and the Elbe—are all in Western Europe.

[7] General Eisenhower dared to launch the D-Day invasion only after his weather intelligence officer was able to tell him that there was a good chance that the prevailing bad weather would break for a short while.

[8] To determine, for instance, how many tanks can cross over the area before their treads turn it into an impassable quagmire.

[9] Product is usually not raw intelligence, but the estimates and conclusions drawn from it.

Freedonia: Army Intelligence, Naval Intelligence, Air Force Intelligence, Coast Guard Intelligence, the Signal Intelligence Service, State Department Intelligence, Customs Service Intelligence, Post Office Intelligence, and the Special Branch of the Freedonian National Police. Some of these agencies have mainly internal functions, while the FIB has none, which is to say that they perform the **counterintelligence** job of keeping track of enemy spies on the homefront and preventing sabotage and subversion. The FIB takes the product from all these diverse sources and from its own operations section, and then its analysis section produces the Freedonian Intelligence Estimate (FIE), from which the president of Freedonia and the Ministry of Foreign Affairs make policy decisions.

Under your direction, the Freedonian Intelligence Bureau takes over a large building in the Freedonian capital city, or builds one of its own, and puts up a large sign over the door that says FREEDONIAN DEPARTMENT OF AGRICULTURE, and erects a double barbed wire fence around the building, and has armed guards, with dogs, patrolling the grounds (which causes some questions). Inside, the building is divided into different areas of interest, known as **desks**. There is a Soviet desk, a French desk, a German desk, and a Sylvanian desk, and so on. Somewhere in the lovely, rolling countryside outside the capital, the Freedonian school for intelligence officers is established. The sign on its lawn reads KING LUDWIG HOME FOR THE CRIMINALLY INSANE, and nobody questions the fence around the property.

You, as spymaster general, sit on the Freedonian Security Council, a body which gives the president advice on international policy. The president, of course, is the ultimate consumer of intelligence; in addition to the FIB, he receives a daily intelligence report and periodic briefings from you and various experts.

In those countries around the world from which Freedonia needs covert intelligence, the FIB has **stations**, each headed by a **chief of station**, which are usually but not always associated with the embassy. In a large or important country, there may also be several outstations, called **bases**, each with its own base chief, which report to the station. Under the chief of station are the **case officers**, who are Freedonian nationals, probably graduates of the King Ludwig Home for the Criminally Insane. Their job is to run **agents**, who may be from any country, or possibly to handle officials of the host country who have been turned around, and are now secretly working for the FIB.

You will have **agents in place**, who have responsible jobs in the target country and have been there a while. These may be walk-in agents, people in the military, government, or even secret service[10] of the target country who have walked into your offices and volunteered their services for personal reasons. If they are from Freedonia, but were planted in the target country many years ago and left alone for all this time, they are **sleeper**

---

[10]   In which case, of course, they are double agents. If they are in place for a while without being used, and so dig their way deeper into the enemy's secret service, they are **moles**.

WANTED
GERMAN SABOTEUR

Courtesy of CULVER PICTURES

Photo taken February 19, 1936

WALTER KAPPE, alias Walter Kappel

F.P.C. 16 M 28 W OOI
M 8 W III

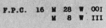

Walter Kappe is known to be connected with sabotage activities being promoted by the Nazi Government. He was born January 12, 1905 at Alfeld, Leina, Germany, and entered the United States on March 9, 1925. He filed application for United States citizenship at Kankakee, Illinois, in June, 1935. He is known to be a member of the German Literary Club, Cincinnati, Ohio, and the Teutonia Club, Chicago, Illinois. Kappe was an agent in the United States for the Ausland Organization and editor "Deutscher Weckruf und Beobachter", official organ of the German-American Bund. Kappe left the United States in 1937 and may return to the United States as an agent for Germany. This individual is described as fol-

HARRIS & EWING

agents, until they are activated. The **agents of influence** are agents who are in a position to influence the policy of the target country, and are used primarily for this purpose rather than for gathering information.

Agents provocateurs are usually used in counterintelligence, or in police work in countries that allow this sort of thing. They pretend to be part of the gang in opposition to the government, but really work for the police. They try to get the gang to do something stupid enough to get itself arrested.[11]

---

11   The Ochrana, the tsar's secret service, was big on agents provocateurs. Its agents would convince groups of liberal students that the only way to relieve the oppressive conditions in Russia was to assassinate the tsar. Then they would capture the students, to show the tsar how necessary the Ochrana was for his safety. Using this technique, it grew to be very large.

Each station will also have its own cipher clerks, and possibly its own communications network separate from that of the embassy. Various experts, on such things as weapons, surveillance, bugging or debugging, papers and documents, or whatever is necessary, will be available to the station chief as needed.

The job of the well-trained FIB case officer will be to develop and **run** networks of agents within the target country. This is done in a hierarchal manner, for everyone's protection. The case officer may work through a **resident agent**, who actually lives in the target country, or in a convenient third country. From the resident, the chain goes to one or more **cut-outs**, or **principal agents**, who serve to further isolate the case officer from the working agent.[12] More separation is obtained by using couriers, and such devices as **dead-drops**, secret places where information and instructions can be left for later retrieval. Dead-drops are very popular and useful, and the first job of a new case officer is to wander around his territory and line up a couple of dozen.[13]

As spymaster general, you create the Freedonian Signal Intelligence Service, or FSIS, a separate organization that passes information to the FIB, has its own network of stations circling enemy territory and such other parts of the world as are of interest to Freedonia. It is responsible for **Communications Intelligence**, as well as **Signal Intelligence**, and quite possibly Electronic Intelligence also. Communications Intelligence, or **COMINT**, is what Secretary Stimson called "reading other people's mail," which these days includes shortwave radio, telephone, microwave, satellite, and other means of transmission. The communications can take the form of voice, teletype, facsimile, binary data, television, or all sorts of multiplexed[14] signals. A small fleet of intelligence-gathering ships, under the command of the Freedonian Navy but in the service of the FSIS, supplements the ground stations.

Much of this information is encrypted. Some codes (it is a closely-guarded secret which ones) have been broken by the FSIS **cryptanalysts**, but many have not, so Signal Intelligence, or **SIGINT**, studies what information can be garnered from the radio signal itself. The FSIS SIGINT people have Direction Finding, or DF, stations set up to triangulate the location of the transmitter. They have delicate "radio fingerprinting" instruments that can take the electronic picture of the signal and tell amazing things about the transmitter and the people using it.

Electronic Intelligence, or ELINT, is the gathering of information about the subject's non-communications-type radio usage, such as radar, of which there are many different types in constant use. These range from the tiny, very short-range sets in the nose cones of ground-to-air or air-to-air missiles, to the huge, over-the-horizon installations that sit in lonely

---

[12]   An agent may see his case officer only once or twice a year—in some cases, much less often. This is necessary for the agent's safety, although it presents the danger of constant psychological strain.

[13]   For an ex-Soviet spy's comments on dead-drops, turn to p. 131.

Courtesy of the New York Public Library Collection

Waite in The London Daily Sketch

"Tell the President his ball is behind the oak, 50 yards past the green."

splendor at the edges of continents and detect incoming ICBMs and enemy bombers.

The Freedonian Air Force has specially equipped spy aircraft, besides running an extensive Freedonian spy satellite program, with which you will keep close watch on potential enemies throughout the world. The satellites perform electronic eavesdropping, as well as photo intelligence **(PHOTINT)**. Up until the mid-1970s, the satellites used film cameras, and ejected pods of film on command, to be swept up by high-flying aircraft trailing scoops. But when a satellite ran out of film, there was no way to reload the cameras, so now they employ very high quality digital processors, like single-frame television cameras, but with a much finer scan. At least once every few hours one of the satellites will be over every spot on the face of the Earth, and can take its picture.

The intelligence agencies of the major countries are now spending vast sums of money on technological means of information collecting—spy satellites, sophisticated information-collecting aircraft and ships, and electronic listening stations—and collect vast amounts of ELINT, COMINT, and PHOTINT. They have huge analysis sections to make sense out of the

14   Multiplexed means "added together." Many digital signals such as teletype or data can be mixed together and sent out on the same frequency, to be unsorted at the other end. Although you must have the proper equipment to unscramble the mess, it is not a form of encryption.

mountains of tape and acres of photographs they produce, and they have scored some signal successes.

As a result, the importance of human intelligence, or **HUMINT**, has been downgraded in the past couple of decades, perhaps more so in the United States than elsewhere. This is generally credited to the American love of gadgets and belief in the fallibility of human agents—the old, sneaky feeling that spying is dirty work, so anyone who does it isn't to be trusted.

But photographs can lie, and photo interpreters can be fooled; radio intercepts can mislead, and the whole rest of the panoply of gadgets may be turned by the enemy to convince us of the reality of some vast deception. It has happened before.[15]

For instance, a satellite can photograph the 200-car train in snaking its way west, toward the border between Sylvania and Freedonia, and a photo interpreter can determine that those cars are usually used to transport infantry. But only a train watcher on the ground can verify that the cars actually hold 5,000 soldiers, and not 100,000 grapefruit. And only an agent highly placed in the enemy government or general staff can tell you whether the moving battalion is going to a rest area or preparing to attack the eastern border of Freedonia.

Technical means of intelligence collection can reveal a fair amount about a target's intentions, but only in dangerously vague terms. PHOTINT can discover that the Sylvanian tank battalions are equipped with river-crossing snorkels, although the only rivers are in Freedonia, but only deep human penetration—say a spy on the enemy's General Staff—can tell whether that is because Sylvanian doctrine is to fight on Freedonian territory if attacked, or to attack next Tuesday.

And a miscalculation on this could start—or lose—a war.

There's no question that it's easier to trust a spy satellite than a spy. And if a spy satellite fails to report it's because a battery went dead, not because it's been apprehended and executed by the enemy. Many spies have been captured and shot, many have been turned, and many have been tricked into sending false information. But for all of that, one spy in the right place is worth a division—sometimes an entire army.

---

[15]   To convince the Germans that the invasion of the continent was going to take place anywhere but where it did, the Allies conceived *Fortitude*, a plan that created the notional (phony) British 4th Army, of 350,000 notional men, complete with cardboard guns, rubber tanks and trucks, but a real radio net, supposedly preparing to invade Norway. The First United Sates Army Group (FUSAG), with 50 notional divisions totalling a million notional men, was notionally getting ready to invade southern France around the Pas de Calais. This double deception survived air photo reconnaissance, and radio interception, and kept a score of German divisions away from Normandy during the real invasion, saving thousands of lives. The fact that Germany had no live agents in England to see for themselves might easily have made the difference between success and failure.

ETHICS AND MORALS

Under what conditions is a country justified in using secret agents? And how far is a secret agent justified in going in the pursuit of his or her goals?

The debate on this is still going on, and will probably continue as long as there are arms to wave and mouths to speak. But many of the debaters on all sides of the issue are arguing polemical viewpoints rather than objective reality. Is a government justified in using spies at all? Of course. In the best of all possible worlds it would be both unnecessary and bad manners to snoop on your neighbors. But this is not that world. Dictatorships are often abrupt and arbitrary, and not prone to announce their decision to go to war very long before attacking. And occasionally even democracies have been known to treat their neighbors in an unfriendly manner. Before the event, who would have dreamed that the Soviet Union would have attacked Finland, that Nazi Germany would have attacked Russia, that Japan would have bombed Pearl Harbor, that India would have overrun Goa, or that Argentina would have attacked the Falkland Islands?

Where the line between the moral and the immoral should be drawn is difficult to judge, and each of us would probably place it differently. It is good to fight off a bully, but bad to punch a random stranger in the face. Somewhere between these two acts we each place our line. If it is moral to spy and to "open other people's mail" for the safety of your country and the preservation of your way of life, is it still moral to do so merely to wrest a commercial advantage from another country or, worse yet, another corporation? If it is moral to spy on a potential enemy, is it still moral to spy on a friend? Is it moral to kill enemy soldiers while engaged in espionage? Enemy civilians?

Intelligence services do kill in the course of their clandestine operations. In some cases as by-product, in self-defense, or out of operational necessity for what they judge to be a worthwhile goal. In some cases, in some services, assassination *is* the goal.[16]

In a totalitarian state the morality of the secret police is the morality of the dictator or ruling group. The people are neither informed nor consulted.[17]

---

[16]   The Bulgarian Secret Service is particularly noted for this. They use such esoterica as poison-tipped umbrellas. It is believed that they were involved in the attempt to murder the Pope. Of course, they are surrogates of the **KGB,** the Soviet Secret Police.

[17]   The Russian tradition considers espionage, subversion, and conspiracy as essential branches of government, and secrecy and ruthlessness as essential methods. The American tradition is marked by distaste for espionage and secrecy and nagging conviction that government measures not enacted in the glare of publicity have something immoral about them. Stalin thought it perfectly normal to tell the 18th Congress of the Communist Party in 1939:

   "Our punitive organs and intelligence service no longer have their sharp edge turned to the inside of the country, but to the outside against external enemies."
   —Sanche de Gramont, *The Secret War*

In a democracy, a consensus must be formed. The intelligence service must not violate the morality of the people, as understood by their elected representatives—at least not too often, not too violently, and not so as to get caught doing it. The perceived morality of the people, in regard to its intelligence service, will, however, swing wildly about in response to the latest outrage, the latest threat, and perhaps the latest spy or war movie.

Intelligence organizations are in the unenviable position of never being able to defend themselves. If something goes wrong, as we have seen, they take the blame—sometimes when they are blameless. But if something goes right, if they score a signal victory in the field of espionage, by its very nature they can't tell anyone.

It is a hard and lonely job to be an intelligence officer, as you will discover when you have guided the FIB for a while.

But there is a secret satisfaction in the knowledge of a job well done.

FOREIGN INTELLIGENCE:
THE ETHICS OF THE CRAFT
by
Arthur L. Jacobs

Arthur L. Jacobs was a civil engineer and an attorney, serving in the Department of Justice and the Treasury Department before becoming a career officer in the Central Intelligence Agency. During his 19 years in the CIA he conducted and monitored some of its sensitive operations in this country and abroad. He has written on intelligence matters for several publications. This article appeared, in a slightly altered form, in Freedom at Issue, *May-June 1982.*

It is timely to restate our country's foreign intelligence mission and to affirm that those who serve that mission do so as dedicated professionals, acting within the bounds of constitutional and statutory authority and in accord with an accepted code of ethical standards.

Challenges

The CIA was created in 1947 as a permanent government organization to obtain and coordinate the skills and capabilities necessary to act as the eyes and ears of our nation and its policymakers and to establish a capability for covert action where needed. The external dominant force which then threatened our interests and the hard-won and costly peace ending World War II was the communist monolith. Headed by the USSR, it had hegemony over Eastern Europe and was threatening the rest of Europe and other continents. That monolith now is fractured, although Soviet expansionism endures—military intervention in Afghanistan and non-military intervention in Poland are recent examples.

Now there are new and different forces that endanger our security interests. The two oceans do not provide a barrier against intercontinental missiles capable of wreaking near total destruction of our mainland. Terrorism is conducted intranationally as well as internationally. Drugs from abroad can tear the very fabric of our society and destroy our most precious asset, the young. And we remain critically dependent on foreign imports, most importantly oil and certain minerals.

The vulnerabilities inherent in an open society and democratic government make it even more difficult to protect ourselves against these threats. To meet them, our government needs many skills and capabilities in our diplomatic arm, in our defense establishment, and in our aid, technical assistance, and cultural programs.

We remain, however, most vulnerable to threats which are held in secret from us. We must first detect, identify, and evaluate such secret threats. Early warning has been and must remain the first priority of our foreign intelligence efforts. Only with such intelligence can our government determine whether and how such threats can be met, by overt means if feasible or by covert action where needed and appropriate. Intelligence and covert action were vital in attaining our independence over two hundred years ago and they are equally essential in retaining that freedom and independence now.

An effective intelligence arm can forewarn us of another Pearl Harbor, an embargo of our foreign oil supply, or other dangers. Counterintelligence is also vital to protect our own secrets; and covert action is an optional form of governmental action where overt methods are neither desirable nor feasible.

The critical element in any intelligence service is personnel. They must be trained, skilled, and disciplined. They must, above all, be dedicated if they are to meet the needs of the craft they have chosen, all of its inherent disabilities and risks, and its lack of public recognition. For two centuries we have had and still have honorable men and women prepared to serve their country, often in complete anonymity and at sacrifice to themselves and their families. Nathan Hale was one of the first; Dick Welch and others who even now cannot be named are our recent ones.

To attain and maintain a healthy and capable intelligence service, we require legislation with realistic lines of responsibility to the top of the executive branch and accountability to the Congress. More importantly, the country must have confidence in the integrity of those men and women who conduct intelligence activities on behalf of a citizenry denied knowledge of them, and for whom the president and a few members of Congress stand as surrogates. But oversight committees and a watchdog media cannot produce foreign intelligence or protect secrets. Covert action cannot be conducted on the front page or the TV screen.

Ours is a culture that tends to a "High Noon" syndrome of meeting enemies openly and face-to-face—but much of the world in which we live is addicted to stabs in the back, a world in which undeclared wars are conducted by "volunteers" who use explosives mindlessly against the innocent. These forces must be countered, not by fighting fire with fire, but by preparing ourselves to detect, identify, and neutralize the forces which threaten our existence.

Toward A Code of Ethics

To that end I propose a Credo and a Code of Ethics for the intelligence craft and those who practice it. This code is not meant to be a substitute for their personal and individual ethics but an addition to them. Just as men and women engaged in the practice of law or medicine complement the private standards that enable them to distinguish right from wrong, proper from improper behavior, with the ethical standards of their profession, so can members of the intelligence craft.

No credo or code of ethics for the professional intelligence officer can be created arbitrarily by laws or administrative directives or enforced by punitive action. Rather it must grow out of historical experience that evolves into tradition. It must convey to the users of intelligence, and to the public, the sense of responsibility that members of the intelligence community have to them as well as to their fellow craftsmen. It must assure these groups that the trust of secrecy will not be abused, that the practitioners will remain committed to the ideal of excellence and to pride in work well done.

Only self-discipline can effectively guarantee compliance to a code of ethics. The highest reward will be the recognition and respect of one's peers for a task professionally done; the disesteem of one's colleagues for violations of those same ethics is the most effective penalty. That the intelligence craft may involve the violation of foreign laws presents no paradox so long as the professional conduct of the intelligence officer is within the scope of American law and accords with his personal standards and those of the craft.

There is a risk in codifying ethical concepts; the cold, written words may themselves chill the spirit of ethical responsibility. There are intelligence officers, past and present, who feel that it is not feasible to reduce to writing a code of ethics. I respect that view, but feel equally strongly that those aspiring to a career in intelligence ought to be apprised of what is expected of them beyond technical capability and personal ethics. Unless such a code is reduced to writing, there can be no agreement on its substance. There is the further difficulty of phrasing a code without making it sound self-serving and platitudinous and without a corollary recognition that inevitably there will be some who will violate or deviate from such a code.

There are attributes peculiar to intelligence for which ethical boundaries should be articulated. In the more conventional disciplines of medicine or law there are proscriptions, both statutory and administrative, whose violation carries the risk of criminal penalty or civil liability. Nonetheless there are those in such professions who for reasons of greed or acclaim violate the ethics of their craft. The successful and superior intelligence officer does not receive public recognition, prizes, or concomitant monetary benefits accorded to his peers in other professions. There are subtle satisfactions in intelligence work, however, which stem from the secrecy itself. That secrecy might tempt the undisciplined to stray to—and beyond—the boundaries of proper professional activity. There is also the rarified, often heady, atmosphere of being among the few who know what the public does not know, who participate in actions of which the public is unaware, and contribute, even to a small degree, to decision-making at the highest level of government.

A strong statement of ethical restraints and ideals would act as a brake on the intelligence officer who would consciously or subconsciously be moved to enlarge his contribution to the decision-making process by substituting his personal perceptions of the national interests where they differ from that determined by the policymakers of our government. Similarly, the same ethical standards will demand strictly objective reporting on intelligence operations and their results to bar the influence of known predilections of the recipient users of the intelligence.

The sense of ethical responsibility must prevail from the beginning to the end of the intelligence process, from the collection through the evaluation, the collation, and to the ultimate dissemination to the users of intelligence. It must prevail as well at the command, staff, and operational levels. Perhaps its importance is more evident in the first link in that chain, in the collection from human sources. With few exceptions, the intelligence officer usually acts alone under exclusive contact with a human source. Hence, it may be that his report cannot be independently verified or confirmed. Others must necessarily assume the professional integrity of the first officer in the chain if his contribution is to be given any validity.

Perhaps the two most important reasons for offering a code of ethics for intelligence are (1) to assure the public that their fellow citizens who have chosen to make a career of foreign intelligence have standards that are in the public interest, and (2) to assure them that disciplined and responsible practitioners need not have any conflict between their personal ethics and those dictated by their work. We should not expect infallibility or invariably successful results from intelligence officers. We can expect that they will be thorough professionals who are faithful to the highest standards when they discharge their responsibilities.

The code of ethics which follows represents, I believe, the

consensus of intelligence officers past and present and has evolved over the more than two hundred years of our own history.

The Credo

From the day of his entry on duty, the intelligence officer is a citizen-soldier committed to the fulfillment of the foreign intelligence mission. He believes himself privileged to participate in the accomplishment of that mission and is proud to join a craft which is an inherent right of nation states. He recognizes that he is engaged in work that was vital to the creation of our nation over two hundred years ago. He is aware that in large measure the preservation of our independence, our very existence, and the constitutional rights of his fellow citizens may depend on his contribution.

The foreign intelligence officer is prepared to dedicate himself to the mission of his organization knowing:

- that it may involve the well-being of his country;
- that he must work in anonymity, without public recognition, and with risk to himself, his family, and his future;
- that should the secrecy of his activities be exposed, he may be disavowed by his government,
- that from the day he leaves the foreign intelligence service, he is thereafter bound by his oath of secrecy to protect the knowledge he has acquired during the course of his service.

The foreign intelligence officer takes pride in his craft as one that is honorable and essential to his government and his fellow citizens; he will be content with the rewards of his work and its achievements and the recognition of his fellow craftsmen and women.

The foreign intelligence officer is sensitive to the fact that his activities are not subject to conventional governmental checks, supervision, and evaluation or to public scrutiny. He is aware that the details of his activities are known to few—even within his own organization. He is highly conscious of the critical insights entrusted to him in the accomplishment of his duties and the importance of safeguarding that knowledge, as well as the funds and materiel provided to carry on his work.

Therefore, the foreign intelligence officer has a special responsibility to account fully and truthfully for his activities to those in our government who are authorized to know, and not to abuse or misuse the shield of secrecy to conceal wrongdoings.

A Code of Ethics

The foreign intelligence officer declares to our government and fellow Americans, without reservation or qualification, that in the discharge of his or her professional responsibilities—

1. He will carry out his duties within the Constitution of the United States and the laws enacted thereunder.
2. He will, to the best of his ability, maintain the highest order of professional skills and organization discipline in the execution of the tasks assigned to him.
3. He will carry out his duties without seeking personal gain or advantage by reason of the duties, facilities, funds, and knowledge entrusted to him.
4. He will report and account fully, freely, truthfully, and objectively on the tasks assigned to him, without fear or favor.
5. He will assiduously guard and protect the integrity of his organization, its methods, and sources.
6. He will conduct himself in his personal life in a manner which will not prejudice his organization, his craft and fellow craftsmen, or the facilities entrusted to him.
7. He will not engage in any unauthorized activity.
8. He will provide objective advice and judgment to and through his organization on the feasibility and risks of any task assigned to him.
9. He will execute the tasks assigned to him, without regard to his personal opinion on the merits of the underlying policy and objectives determined to be in the national interest by the authority assigning such tasks.
10. Notwithstanding, he will communicate and report any moral, religious, or ethical reservation or objection to any task assigned to him.
11. He may ask to be relieved of any task or duty assigned to him by reason of such reservation or objection and to

resign from the intelligence service whenever his personal convictions are incompatible with his continued service.

12. He will report any violations of this code to and through command channels and, if necessary, to the inspector general of his organization.

It would be a mistake to single out any one of these precepts as being of greater importance than another, since they are interdependent. But if there is any hallmark of the intelligence officer and his work, it is in an overriding commitment to the truth—the truth he seeks, the truth of his activities, and the truth to himself. If "the truth shall make you free" can be said to be the motto of intelligence, then the work of the intelligence officer can make a vital contribution to keeping us free.

2 RECRUITING THE SPY

The Freedonian Intelligence Bureau needs a few good people. How to get them? You could, of course, put ads in the local papers:[1]

> WANTED—a few highly intelligent, very nosy men and women for interesting work. Must speak fluent Sylvanian, but be native born Freedonians with no close relatives living in Sylvania.

But most intelligence services are leery of doing that. Their attitude seems to be that of Groucho Marx, who refused to join any club that would have him as a member. The thinking is that if one can't apply for the job, then it is impossible for the enemy to sneak a double agent in on you. This logic is, as has been demonstrated time after time, fallacious.[2]

One popular means of recruiting that has shown mixed results is what we might call the "Old Spies' Network."

Retired spies go into a number of professions. Some run for public office.[3] Some become novelists. Some write an endless series of memoirs. Many go into teaching. The man or woman staring down at you from the lecture platform of your local university, trying to ascertain what, if anything, you know about Danton's role in the French Revolution, or asking you to contrast and compare the electoral systems of the Republic of Korea, the Vatican, and the Screen Actors' Guild, may have spent his or her formative years running around some foreign countryside trying to find just one more usable dead drop.[4]

---

[1]   The CIA has been doing just that recently.

[2]   The KGB comes to mind. And the British SIS went through a period after World War II when it seemed like the entire senior staff planned to retire to dachas on the Black Sea.

[3]   In countries which have free elections. Menachem Begin, the ex-prime minister of Israel, for one example, spent some time in the Irgun.

[4]   See chapter 17.

This professorial old spy, a charter member of the Old Spies' Network, will consider it a duty, and a pleasure, to recommend to promising young talent from the classroom that they seriously consider a career of (secret) service to their country.

THE RIGHT PERSON FOR THE RIGHT JOB

A certain number of people are recruited by an intelligence service because they have special knowledge or skills needed by the service. And the special knowledge or skills needed by an intelligence service can be varied and unusual. Carpenters, plumbers, and electricians, as well as programmers, communications specialists, and scientists and technicians of many sorts, are needed, as are tailors, bootmakers, thieves, safecrackers, forgers, and whores (of all sexes). It is said that one British intelligence service kept an astrologer on staff during World War II.[5]

For the specialties, of course, you hire specialists. But what sort of skills should Freedonia demand from its regular agents—its career spies? Who should you recruit for the FIB?

There are five major job classifications in the intelligence business: Counterintelligence Officer, Intelligence Analyst, Case Officer, Operations Officer, and Agent. The qualifications required for each job are different intellectually, physically, and emotionally. A candidate that might be perfect for one job, might well be inefficient, or downright dangerous in another.[6] Let's examine the needs of each job.

The *counterintelligence officer* is essentially a detective, and the skills needed are the same as any police department would require of its detective division. Loyalty, intelligence, great attention to detail, and the almost instinctive ability to notice anything out of the ordinary, will be of great use. A dogged determination, approaching the compulsive, to dig out all the details and completely understand all the ramifications of a given happening would be a good trait. For those counterintelligence officers guarding great secrets or important officials, a fair degree of paranoia is recommended.[7]

Many countries use their police forces for counterintelligence functions,[8] and detectives have often been borrowed when a counterintelligence function is needed by an overseas intelligence service. Both

---

[5]   Hitler believed in astrology, and had a personal astrologer. The British wanted to know what advice der Führer was receiving from the planets.

[6]   Acting on the belief that any officer should be able to do any job, the U.S. Army assigns officers at random to the various intelligence branches for short terms, considering these stepchildren of the "fighting branches" as unworthy to build careers upon. Which is, perhaps, why the term "Army Intelligence" is regarded as an oxymoron.

[7]   There is an old saying in the military to the effect that "Once is happenstance, twice is coincidence, three times is enemy action." Some overzealous counterintelligence

the British SIS and the American CIA have on occasion recruited from their countries' police forces for jobs that needed trained detectives.

The *intelligence analyst* studies a country, or a subject in great depth, using information from both covert and overt sources, and prepares papers from which senior analysts draw up country or area appreciations and politicians make policy decisions. The personality and inclinations of an intelligence analyst parallel those of a college professor, and indeed these two professions have been interchangeable (in the sense that many people have gone from one to the other and back) over the years. A good intelligence analyst is possessed of the kind of intellectual wizardry that enables him or her to take five apparently unrelated facts, and come up with an unexpected—but accurate—conclusion. This is a fascinating career for the sociologist or historian, and enables one to gain insights into human affairs and political behavior that are seldom available to contemporaries. The fact that one is not allowed to discuss these insights, or the facts that led to them, or publish unclassified papers regarding them for at least the next 20 years, has led to great frustration. Imagine having a wonderful toy and being unable to show it to anybody.

The *case officer* is the person in the field who runs agents. He or she must be absolutely reliable, and good at handling people. A quick intelligence and the ability to make decisions would not be amiss, as well as a proficiency with languages and the talent of blending in with his or her surroundings.

The absolute reliability must go in both directions; his superiors must be able to rely on his judgment and his honesty, since he will be responsible for his country's interests, and possibly large sums of unaccountable money or other disbursables.[9] His agents must feel that they can rely completely on him, as he will often be their only link with the country for which they are risking their lives and their only hope for safety, and possibly life itself, if anything goes awry.

The case officer usually recruits the agents in the field. He must be able to judge the degree of dissatisfaction, or greed, in the potential agent, and the worth of the information the agent will be able to supply. He must have the sixth sense that warns him of double agents, or of people so unstable or so involved in their own problems that they will prove more trouble than they're worth to handle. A person who volunteers because he hates the enemy with an undying passion, because the enemy has, perhaps, killed his parents or children, or tortured his wife or lover, is to be pitied, and

---

organizations have modified this to read: "Once is enemy action." This leaves no room for happenstance or coincidence, and may seriously bother foreign journalists and commercial travellers.

[8]   Alan Pinkerton, founder of the Pinkerton Detective Agency, set up and ran the Union counterintelligence service for President Lincoln during the Civil War.

[9]   Some agents demand payment in gold, or stamps, or Swiss bank accounts. Some merely need to know they're loved.

perhaps helped; but he will make an untrustworthy agent because he will see only the worst, and his reports will be colored by his need for revenge.

It is upon the judgment and ability of the case officer, the person in the field, that the success rate and the reputation of an intelligence agency are founded. It is upon the ability of the spymaster general of Freedonia to recruit and hold capable case officers that the safety of his country may depend.

The *operations officer* is the person who works in the Clandestine Operations Section of the Freedonian Intelligence Bureau. The FIB will claim that it doesn't have any such thing as a Clandestine Operations Section, but that will be a fib. No country today, or indeed for the past 3,000 years, can afford to overlook the occasional need for a clandestine operation of some sort. Intelligence agents only gather information. To have them do anything else is to jeopardize their mission, and possibly cut off your supply of information. But sometimes you need someone to *do* something.

The problem presented is the same one that governments and rulers have been facing for many years: If you hire and train someone to break the laws of another country and do nasty things while there, how do you prevent this disdain for the law from following him back to your country when he returns?

The United States has had several recent examples of people who believed that, if they could do something while working for the clandestine section of CIA, then they should be able to do the same things when they leave the Company whether for some Texan, or for Colonel Khaddafi, or for someone who claims to know what the president *really* wants, even if it's illegal.

The code of ethics for the intelligence services proposed by Arthur Jacobs[10] covers this in paragraph 7: "He will not engage in any unauthorized activity."[11]

So, strangely enough, it is in the most secret department of the secret service, the "Department of Dirty Tricks," as it is known in some services, that it is most important to have people with a strong moral sense, and a bit of ethical training. Patriotism would be an excellent virtue for the operations agent, but the word has gone so far out of fashion that anyone who professes it probably has a strong ideological bent that might not be precisely what you have in mind. Someone who sees communists under every bush is of no more use to you than someone who sees capitalists up every tree.

Aside from this caveat, the operations officer should possess those same qualities of intelligence, aptitude, speed of decision making, and linguistic aptitude as the case officer. There may be specific needs, depending on the operation you have in mind.

---

[10]   See pp. 14-21.

[11]   Paragraph one: "He will carry out his duties within the Constitution of the United States and the laws enacted thereunder," should also give these people pause.

Courtesy of CULVER PICTURES

The agent at work.

The *agent* is a different matter. The term is loosely used to mean a spy, and thus anyone in the intelligence field. Certainly anyone in intelligence who doesn't stay at home and work at a desk is considered an agent.

In the more precise terminology of the intelligence specialist, the word "agent" is strictly used to signify the person in the field who is supplying the information. Sometimes the agent is not the initial supplier of the information, but gets it from a source, who may be witting or unwitting. If witting, then the source is also an agent. An agent is usually not picked for any skills he or she might possess, but is chosen by expedience or will volunteer from necessity. An agent can be someone from your country who is planted in the target country, but is more usually a native of the target country or some neutral third country.

The two qualities that make an agent are simply that the prospective agent must have something you want, and must want something you have. The something you want is almost always information or access to information. The something you have could be money, or security, or an interesting sex partner,[12] or pictures of him or her with the interesting sex partner, or a

---

[12]   Blackmail is an age-old tool of the intelligence business. The Germans, the Russians, and the Japanese are famous (in the field) for using sexual coercion and sexual blackmail as tools of the trade.

promise to arrange a defection at the proper time, or just a political system that the agent approves of more than his own (if he is a native of the penetrated country).

Some intelligence services believe in using a few highly-placed agents to develop their information, concentrating on staff officers, cabinet ministers, important businessmen and the like. Others use a swarm of low-level agents, recruiting every chambermaid, valet, desk clerk, taxi driver, barber, hair dresser, manicurist, hooker, and garbageman they can find. It becomes generally known, for example, among the native populations living around American military bases in foreign (usually, but not always, third world) countries that small but meaningful sums of money can be had by anyone bringing any information about the Americans to a certain address. As a result, the native garbagemen put aside the American garbage for later sorting through, the native barbers listen closely when they cut American hair, and the ladies of the night are paying attention to more than one business when they have an American client.

QUALITIES OF A SECRET AGENT— CIRCA 1910

Hugh Morrice—as he here prefers to call himself—is in many ways a very remarkable man—a veritable prince of secret agents. For years he has been one of my most intimate friends, and often my fellow-traveller across Europe. An accomplished linguist, a brilliant raconteur, a good all-around sportsman, a polished diplomat, a born adventurer, a cosmopolitan of cosmopolitans, still under forty, and a personal friend of half-a-dozen reigning sovereigns, it was declared of him by the German Imperial Chancellor not long ago that he knew more of the Continent, and of the under-currents of international politics, than any other living man. Many a time has secret information supplied by him, turned the tide of political events in Great Britain's favour.

As much at home in any European city of importance as in his own snug rooms off Piccadilly, or in his thatched country cottage in Sussex, he possesses an enormous circle of friends, both official and unofficial, yet as secret agent of the British Government abroad he is amazingly elusive, ever evading detection or betrayal, and at the same time astoundingly successful in ascertaining the secrets of other nations which our authorities desire to know.

Exceedingly modest and retiring he hates the lime-light of publicity, and half his time lives in seclusion under a fictitious name. I have encountered him in all sorts of odd and unexpected places, and in all sorts of guises. So clever and cautious is he to conceal his identity that not a soul outside the small circle of his own colleagues at Whitehall is aware of his real profession or of the great secrets of State with which he is so constantly entrusted. The shrewdness, tact and courage he displays are surely unequalled, while the high appreciation in which our late Sovereign held his many services to diplomacy and to the nation has been shown by the special honours conferred upon him, and the large grants he has, on several occasions, received from the Secret Service Fund.

That his wandering, erratic life is daily crowned by romance and stirring adventure is plainly shown in these chapters of exciting incident which I have written down at his dictation between deep whiffs at his pipe, and here venture to present in narrative form.

William Le Queux
Devonshire Club, London

From *Revelations of the Secret Service*
by William Le Queux

THE RIGHT MACHINE . . .

Increasingly, the intelligence services of the richer countries are relying on sophisticated electronic means for collection of intelligence. Spy satellites capable of reading the license plates of ground cars relay pictures of ground targets. Delicate radio ears on satellites and at the borders of countries listen to the country's secret communications. Great computers work day and night to break the codes of other countries.

But even these technical means of collection require the services of human beings, and a better trained, more knowledgeable human being than ever before. As long as one country feels it necessary to hide information from another, and the other country feels threatened by it, just so long will spying continue. The means will change, the personnel needs will change, but the great game—as espionage was called by certain practitioners in the 19th century—will go on.

3 SELF TEST FOR SPIES

You now have a host of recruits to man the FIB, but before you assign them to jobs, you, as spymaster general, should determine whether or not these recruits have the right stuff.

How do you do that, you might ask. And how, for that matter, do you determine your own qualifications to serve as spymaster general?

Following is a self-test. If you take it honestly and objectively, it will give you a good idea of the stuff that makes a good spy and, more importantly, a good spymaster general.

THE TEST

Answer the questions as honestly as possible, but temper your honesty with common sense. One of the questions, for example, is whether you like and regularly go to the opera. If you like the opera, live in a small town in Nebraska, and look forward to your annual visits to New York so you can go to the opera, then the answer is yes even though you only go once a year. In the first part (the personal stuff), remember that this is for you only, and be honest even if you think you know the answer wanted. If an intelligence agency is ever testing you they won't rely on your answers for the truth.

Try to do the whole written part of the test at one sitting. Number from 1 to 41 on a separate piece of paper, and fill in your answers. There is no time limit, but keep track of how long you take. The answers, the scoring, and an explanation will be found on pp. 36-40.

PERSONAL

1. You are regarded as
    (a) highly attractive
    (b) fairly attractive
    (c) average
    (d) fairly plain looking
    (e) ugly

2. You are
    (a) brilliant
    (b) fairly intelligent
    (c) average
    (d) not too smart
    (e) dumb

3. Your physical condition is
    (a) Olympic caliber
    (b) fine, and you work at it
    (c) good for a once-a-week exerciser
    (d) okay
    (e) not discussed

4. You regard yourself as a leader [yes/no].

5. You regard yourself as a follower [yes/no].

6. You have a strong and positive sense of morality, which your minister/priest/rabbi would approve of [yes/no].

7. You have a strong, but unconventional, sense of morality based upon your own readings and beliefs [yes/no].

8. You believe that there are times when morality of any sort should give way to expedience [yes/no].

9. You:
    (a) like to gossip and can't keep a secret for more than a minute.
    (b) like to gossip, but can keep a secret for days at a time
    (c) can keep a secret if required
    (d) have no difficulty keeping a secret
    (e) have never been told a secret

10. Of those listed, your favorite sport is
    (a) baseball
    (b) tennis
    (c) football
    (d) hockey
    (e) polo

11. You would least like to be suddenly thrust:
    (a) into a strange city
    (b) into a strange small town
    (c) into a strange forest
    (d) onto a strange desert

12. Which description fits you best?
    (a) You fall in love easily, as you have proven many times.
    (b) You don't fall in love easily, but when you do it is an all-controlling passion.

    (c) You seldom fall in love, but enjoy the favors of the opposite (or the same, if you swing that way) sex when they are offered.

    (d) You have never fallen in love.

13. And speaking of sex:
    (a) You are exclusively heterosexual.
    (b) You are exclusively homosexual.
    (c) You are usually heterosexual.
    (d) You are usually homosexual.
    (e) You are bisexual.
    (f) You haven't figured out yet just what you are.

NOT SO PERSONAL

14. In addition to English, you are completely fluent in the following languages: _____, _____, _____.

15. You are proficient (black belt or the equivalent) in the following martial arts: _____, _____.

16. You can proficiently _____drive a car, _____fly a small plane, _____fly a multi-engined plane, _____sail a boat, _____pilot a powerboat.

17. You are really fond of and good at (check all that apply): _____chess, _____bridge, _____poker, _____crossword puzzles, _____acrostics.

18. You enjoy (check all that apply): _____swimming, _____horseback riding, _____riflery, _____archery, _____fishing, _____hunting, _____skiing.

19. You have a pistol and a belt or shoulder holster, and you practice quick-draw shooting [yes/no].

20. Which magazines do you read regularly?

21. Which newspapers do you read regularly?

22. You like and regularly go to (check all that apply): _____movies, _____foreign films, _____plays, _____opera, _____ballet, _____modern dance, _____discos, _____poetry recitals.

23. How many books do you read a month?

24. How many places more than 100 miles away from home have you visited in the past two years (do not count business travel unless you are self-employed)?

25. How many of these places were out of the country?

GENERAL KNOWLEDGE

26. Identify with a short sentence each of the following people:
    (a) William Rehnquist
    (b) Henry L. Stimson
    (c) Margaret Thatcher
    (d) William J. Donovan
    (e) Donald E. Westlake

27. Identify with a short sentence each of the following places:
    (a) Runnymede
    (b) Alamogordo
    (c) Versailles
    (d) Erewhon
    (e) Thermopylae

28. Write down the names of as many of the 50 states as you can think of.

29. Now the names of as many of the first 40 presidents as you can think of, in as close to sequential order as you can manage.

30. Identify the following:
    (a) isobar
    (b) MIG 24
    (c) sidewinder
    (d) GNP
    (e) Mossad

31. Identify the following:
    (a) amino acid
    (b) DNA
    (c) the Big Bang
    (d) MOSFET
    (e) $299,792$ or $186,282$

32. And yet again identify the following:
    (a) *Voyager*
    (b) *Sputnik*
    (c) *Apollo 13*
    (d) *Greenpeace*
    (e) *The Argo*

NOW TO SPECIFICS

33. Identify in one sentence:
    (a) sleeper
    (b) turned around
    (c) station
    (d) desk
    (e) cut out

34. Name the main intelligence service of each of these countries:
    - (a) United States
    - (b) Soviet Union
    - (c) Great Britain
    - (d) South Korea
    - (e) Israel

35. Name the main counterintelligence service of each of these countries:
    - (a) United States
    - (b) Soviet Union
    - (c) Great Britain
    - (d) France
    - (e) West Germany

36. What is a:
    - (a) book code
    - (b) substitution cipher
    - (c) transposition cipher
    - (d) Vigenère table
    - (e) Playfair cipher

37. The five most common letters in English language text are ____, ____, ____, ____, and ____.

38. Identify:
    - (a) ELINT
    - (b) SIGINT
    - (c) COMINT
    - (d) PHOTINT
    - (e) HUMINT

39. Decode this most dangerous message:

```
OJ ZDIS FZJPJ FWRFZP FD MJ PJIL-JEASJBF FZKF KII YJB KWJ VWJKFJS

JCRKI FZKF FZJT KWJ JBSDOJS MT FZJAW VWJKFDW OAFZ VJWFKAB

RBKIAJBKMIJ WANZFP FZKF KYDBN FZJPJ KWJ IALJ IAMJWFT KBS FZJ

XRWPRAF DL ZKXXABJPP -- FZKF FD PJVRWJ FZJPJ WANZFP NDEJWBYJBFP

KWJ ABPFAFRFJS KYDBN YJB SJWAEABN FZJAW GRPF XDOJWP LWDY FZJ

VDBPJBF DL FZJ NDEJWBJS FZKF OZJBJEJW KBT LDWY DL NDEJWBYJBF

MJVDYJP SJPFWRVFAEJ DL FZJPJ JBSP AF AP FZJ WANZF DL FZJ XJDXIJ

FD KIFJW DW FD KMDIAPZ AF KBS FD ABPFAFRFJ BJO NDEJWBYJBF IKTABN

AFP LDRBSKFADB DB PRVZ XWABVAXIJP KBS DWNKBAQABN AFP XDOJWP AB

PRVZ LDWY KP FD FZJY PZKII PJJY YDPF IAHJIT FD JLLJVF FZJAW

PKLJFT KBS ZKXXABJPP.
```

NOW THE PHYSICAL STUFF

40. Go out in the world and follow a random stranger to his destination. Try to discover his (or her) name, occupation, and both home and

business address. Try not to be spotted or get arrested. Under no conditions approach this stranger.

41. Locate five dead-drops (see p. 131) within walking distance, if possible. Put a dollar bill in each. Go back two weeks later and see how many dollars you still have.

THE TEST ANSWERS

1. Give yourself three points if you answered "c"—average looking—and take one point off for each step away, in either direction. An agent should always blend in with his background.

2. Three points if you're brilliant, two if you're fairly intelligent, and none below that. You had better be smarter than the people trying to catch you, and they're going to be better than average.

3. Three points for (a) or (b), and if you're below that, you'd better work at it. A sluggish agent is a dead agent.

4. Two points for no.

5. Two points for no. A spy is a loner, an observer, who only leads when being chased and never follows.

6. No points for this. If the answer was no, keep going. If the answer was yes, you would be a very dangerous agent to yourself and those around you. This is not a comment on religion, but on the sort of rigid positiveness that would enable you to answer the question "yes." Your minister/priest/rabbi probably has moral questions. Why don't you?

7. Two points for a yes. Spies should consider moral questions—should be aware that they exist.

8. No points. If you said yes, you flunk.

9. Review your answer now and see if it rings true. Two points for (c), and one point for answering honestly.

10. Two points for baseball or tennis, which are, in their own way, individual sports. A spy must enjoy being an individual. Nothing for football or hockey. If you said polo, one point for swank.

11. No points, but if any of the possibilities gave you a second of serious worry, perhaps you should reconsider your career goals, since all are possible if you become an agent.

12. Three points for either (a) or (c), no points for (b) or (d). You must be a man/woman who is in control, even in passion. If you've never been in love, you're either dangerously sexually repressed[1] or one day you're

---

[1]   Excuse the pop psychology, this is only a test.

going to completely flip over someone who is probably an enemy agent.

13. No points for this one, either, since it shouldn't matter to anyone but you and your partner. But if you found yourself not wanting to answer, for whatever reason, you might be subject to blackmail, and therefore shouldn't have access to any of your country's secrets.

14. Three points for each language up to three. An extra point for each one where the natives would think you're a native (up to a total of 12).

15. Three points for each art, up to two. If you spend more than six hours a week practicing, take a point off.

16. Two points for each.

17. Give yourself a point for each one you're really interested in, two points for each one you are really good at, and three points for each (except crosswords or acrostics) you are a master of.

18. Two points for each, and an extra point for fishing. It has been said that the fisherman has the perfect psychological makeup for espionage: patience, skill, and an absorbing interest in minutiae.

19. No points. If yes, disqualify yourself. You do not have the right sort of personality for subtle, unobtrusive work.

20. Disregarding *TV Guide* and *Cable Week*, and others of such ilk, two points for each magazine, three for each science or economics magazine (up to 12 points).

21. Two points for each newspaper (up to 8 points).

22. One point for each.

23. One point for each over five for a maximum of five points.

24. Two points for each. You must enjoy travel, you'll be doing a lot of it.

25. Two extra points for each (up to a total of 12 points for these two questions).

26. Two points for each, if you said they were (a) chief justice of the Supreme Court, (b) the secretary of state who said "Gentlemen do not read other people's mail,"[2] (c) prime minister of Great Britain (not England), (d) chief of the OSS, (e) contemporary American novelist.

27. Two points for each, if you said they were (a) where the *Magna Charta* was signed, (b) the site in New Mexico where the first atomic device was exploded, (c) the palace, right outside of Paris, where the various Louis reigned, (d) the mythical land in the utopian novel by Samuel

---

[2] The guy was mentioned three times already in this book. A spy must have a good head for detail.

Butler, (e) the rocky pass where Leonidas and his Spartans, Thebans, and Thespians held off the Persian invaders in 480 B.C.[3]

28. Five points if you got all 50. One point off for each one you missed.[4]

29. Five points if you got all 40. One point off for each one you missed. An extra 5 if you got any ten in the right order.[5]

30. Two points each for (a) a line on a weather map connecting places having the same barometric pressure, (b) a modern Russian fighter plane, (c) an American air-to-air missile,[6] (d) abbreviation for Gross National Product: the total value of the goods and services produced in one year, (e) the Israeli secret service.

31. Two points each for: (a) the basic building blocks of protein, (b) the molecule that encodes the genetic structure of life, (c) the theory that the universe was formed in one instant, (d) Metal Oxide Semiconductor Field Effects Transistor,[7] (e) the speed of light in a vacuum in kilometers per second and miles per second.[8]

32. Two points each for: (a) either one of the two unmanned space explorers, or the round-the-world-without-stopping aircraft,[9] (b) the Russian satellite that got there first, (c) the U.S. mission to the Moon that had to come home for repairs, (d) the international organization that doesn't like whalers or atomic submarines, (e) the ship, in Greek mythology, that Jason sailed off on.

33. Two points each for (a) an agent in storage and in place for future use, (b) one of their men who is secretly working for you, (c) the head office of an intelligence agency in a foreign country, (d) the location in the headquarters at home where that foreign country is studied, (e) someone who separates an agent from his case officer for reasons of security.

34. Two points each for: (a) the CIA, (b) the KGB, (c) MI.6 or SIS, (d) the KCIA, (e) the Mossad.

---

[3]   And where the Anzacs held off the German Army in April 1941, but no extra points.

[4]   Alabama, Alaska, Arizona, Arkansas, California, Colorado, Connecticut, Delaware, Florida, Georgia, Hawaii, Idaho, Illinois, Indiana, Iowa, Kansas, Kentucky, Louisiana, Maine, Maryland, Massachusetts, Michigan, Minnesota, Mississippi, Missouri, Montana, Nebraska, Nevada, New Hampshire, New Jersey, New Mexico, New York, North Caroliina, North Dakota, Ohio, Oklahoma, Oregon, Pennsylvania, Rhode Island, South Carolina, South Dakota, Tennessee, Texas, Utah, Vermont, Virginia, Washington, West Virginia, Wisconsin, Wyoming.

[5]   And they are:
      George Washington, John Adams, Thomas Jefferson, James Madison, James Monroe, John Quincy Adams, Andrew Jackson, Martin Van Buren, William Henry Harrison, John Tyler, James Knox Polk, Zachary Taylor, Millard Fillmore, Franklin Pierce, James Buchanan, Abraham Lincoln, Andrew Jackson, Ulysses Simpson Grant, Rutherford B.

35. Two points each for: (a) the FBI, (b) the KGB, (c) MI.5, (d) the SDECE, (e) the BfV.

36. Two points each for (a) a word-substitution code kept in a book, or using a book, (b) a cipher where a letter outside the message is substituted for one in the message, (c) a cipher where the letters in the message are mixed up, (d) a method of encrypting by substitution cipher, (e) cipher used by the British during the World Wars.

37. One point each for E, T, A, O, N.

38. Two points each for: (a) Electronics Intelligence, (b) Signal Intelligence, (c) Communications Intelligence, (d) Photographic Intelligence, (e) Human Intelligence.

39. Only five points, its length only makes it easier. If you have it, you'll know.

40. and 41. Ten points each for succeeding.

WHAT DOES ALL THIS MEAN?

The top score is something over 250. Score yourself this way:

200+: You have a natural aptitude and all the right interests. Call the recruiter.

150-200: See what you're soft in, but they'll probably send you to school for it, so call the recruiter.

100-150: If you are very strong in one particular skill or bit of knowledge, like some obscure language, or you have the ability to cloud men's minds so they cannot see you, then call the recruiter. If not, good luck.

Below 100: Your mother always wanted you to be a doctor or an accountant anyway. Listen to your mother.

Many of the questions on this test were random shots, of necessity, because we couldn't give you an all-day test. What we were looking for was

---

Hayes, James Abram Garfield, Chester Alan Arthur, Grover Cleveland, Benjamin Harrison, Gover Cleveland, William McKinley, Theodore Roosevelt, William Howard Taft, Woodrow Wilson, Warren G. Harding, Calvin Coolidge, Herbert Clark Hoover, Franklin D. Roosevelt, Harry S. Truman, Dwight David Eisenhower, John F. Kennedy, Lyndon Baines Johnson, Richard Milhous Nixon, Gerald R. Ford, Jimmy Carter, Ronald W. Reagan

[6] One point for the snake.

[7] "A transistor" is acceptable.

[8] Only two points even if you got both.

[9] Five points for both.

general aptitude, intelligence, and a naturally enquiring mind. And besides, many intelligence services have vastly different standards. Don't forget: There *are* other countries besides Freedonia.

Good luck, however you did.

4 ORGANIZATIONS

Every good spymaster should know the names, and some of the history, of the more important or more notorious spy organizations of the past and present. Besides, throwing around a few appropriate names in conversation is an easy way to seem like an expert. So here is a brief country-by-country listing of what some of the competition is, and what it has been.[1]

The accuracy of these reports cannot be guaranteed. In some cases, the country concerned has never officially admitted that the organization named actually exists or existed. The order is alphabetical by country.

FRANCE

The Deuxième Bureau is the intelligence division of the French General Staff.[2] The actual military secret service is the Service de Renseignements, which is the Cinquième Bureau. The Deuxième Bureau has had its ups and downs over the years. Totally discredited at the turn of the century by the Dreyfus affair,[3] it slowly rebuilt its reputation until, after World War I, it was held in high regard in Britain and Germany. World War II showed this regard to be perhaps undeserved.

---

[1]   For a few names that aren't on this list, see the Glossary.

[2]   The Belgians, Czechs, and Poles also have or had Deuxième Bureaux.

[3]   Captain Albert Dreyfus of the French Army was convicted of treason in December 1894, on evidence manufactured by the Deuxième Bureau to cover up its own errors and those of the General Staff. He was selected for this honor principally because he was a Jew. After five years on Devil's Island, and another six years during which the army knew him to be innocent but refused to admit it (the real traitor, a Major Esterhazy, fled to England in 1898), his conviction was finally quashed and he was reinstated in the army with the rank of major. Emile Zola, the famous French novelist, wrote an editorial headlined "J'accuse," accusing the government of complicity in Dreyfus's unjust court-martial. Zola was prosecuted for his trouble and sentenced to a year in prison (the sentence was reversed at the last moment).

The SDECE, the Service de Documentation Extérieure et de Contre-Espionage, is the French foreign intelligence service.

The BCRA, the Bureau Central de Renseignements et d'Action, was the intelligence organization of General Charles de Gaulle during the Second World War.

The OAS, Organisation de l'Armeé Secrète, was the secret organization of French Army officers set up in 1961 by General Raoul Salan. It conspired, but failed, to destroy the Algerian independence movement.

GERMANY

West German intelligence is handled by the Federal Intelligence Agency or BND (Bundesnachrichtendienst), which was founded in 1956 and headed by Reinhard Gehlen until 1968.

The counterintelligence agencies are the BfV or Bundesamt für Verfassungsschutz, the state office for the defense of the constitution, which is the equivalent of the FBI, but has no powers of arrest, and the MAD or Militärischer Abschirmdienst, which is responsible for CI within the armed forces.

The SSD, the Staatssicherheitsdienst (State Security Service), is the *East* German political police.

The Abwehr was the intelligence and counterintelligence service of the German General Staff. During World War II it was headed by the famous Admiral Canaris, who was an anti-Nazi and was hung by the Nazis in late 1944 for plotting against Hitler. The organization survived him by only a few months.

B-Dienst, Beobachtung-Dienst, was the German cryptanalysis section charged with naval ciphers during World War II.

Forschungsamt was the name of Reichsmarschall Goering's Luftwaffe Secret Service.

The Gestapo, the name abbreviated from Geheime Staatspolizei (literally, "Secret State Police"), was the purely Nazi organization for internal security and external espionage and sabotage. One of the few secret services with its own uniform, the Gestapo was known for the utter ruthlessness and brutality of its agents.

The RSHA, Reichssicherheitshauptamt (the "Reich Main Security Office"), was formed in 1939, and controlled the Gestapo, the criminal police, and the SD.

The SD, Sicherheitsdienst, was the security department of the SS charged with political intelligence and espionage.

GREAT BRITAIN

GCHQ, Government Communication Headquarters, is the British codebreaking organization. Originally known as GC&CS,[4] the Government

---

4   A direct outgrowth of the famous Admiralty codebreaking section known as "Room 40" in World War I.

Courtesy of the New York Public Library Collection

"Anybody here from M.I.5 . . .
Anybody here from M.I.5 . . ."

Code and Cipher School, it changed its name and began operating out of Bletchley Park, an estate in Buckinghamshire, from September 1939. Its success in breaking the German "Enigma" cipher, the principal cipher machine used by the Germans during World War II, produced "Ultra" intelligence. Its dissemination restricted to a very few, Ultra gave the Allies a close-to-unbeatable edge in the war in Europe.

MI.5, also called the Security Service, is the counterintelligence service of Great Britain. It was headed by Major-General Sir Vernon Kell from its beginning in 1909 when it was known as MO.5. Kell served for 31 years until he was replaced by Sir David Petrie in 1940. During World War II it captured and "turned" every Nazi agent landed in Great Britain, and had over 40 of them feeding false information to the Abwehr and the Gestapo until the end of the war.

MI.6, also known as the Secret Intelligence Service, or SIS, was founded in 1909, along with MI.5, after the Boer War had shocked the British government into realizing that, aside from some agents in places Britain took a paternal, if imperial, interest in, like India and Ireland, it had no people in place anywhere in the world.[5] The SIS quickly established a reputation of almost supernatural ability. This reputation, although totally undeserved, proved useful during and after World War II. The SIS has had many successes which, of course, it cannot talk about, but its record was marred by a series of defections after the war, when several high-ranking officers proved to have been moles for the Soviet Union. Perhaps the most famous of these is Kim Philby.

Other MI.'s, in existence during World War II, were: MI.8, the Signals Intelligence Service; MI.9, the Escape and Evasion Service; and MI.11, which was in charge of "black" propaganda.

The PID is the Political Intelligence Division of Her Britannic Majesty's Foreign Office. Its job is to supply intelligence and national estimates to the Cabinet.

The SOE, the Special Operations Executive, was founded in 1940. Originally in two branches—SO1, which handled propaganda to enemy-occupied territories (later renamed Political Warfare Executive [PWE]), and SO2, operations—its purpose was to support and coordinate resistance to the Axis powers in all the occupied countries of Europe, or, as Winston Churchill put it, to "set Europe ablaze!"

The Special Branch of Scotland Yard has both intelligence and counterintelligence functions.

ISRAEL

The Mossad—short for Mossad Letafkidim Meyouchadim,[6] the Israeli Intelligence Service—is the principal external intelligence organization of

---

[5]   Its secret was well kept. The myth of British Secret Service omniscience was strong in foreign capitals even then.

[6]   There is also the Mossad Bitachon Leumi, the Central Insitute for Intelligence, but it is

the state of Israel. It was founded in 1951, and in less than half a century has earned the reputation of being one of the four best intelligence services in the world.[7]

The Irgun was a sabotage group that was dedicated to ending the British partition of Palestine. During World War II it was in the difficult position of being both anti-German and anti-British.

Shai was the intelligence section of the Haganah, the secret army of Israel during the years before it was recognized as a state.

Shin Beth is the internal security force of Israel.

ITALY

The Italian intelligence organization during World War II was the Servizio Internazionale Militare, known as SIM. Headed by General Cesare Amé, their big success was the copying of the "Black Code" from the American Embassy. This code, as recovered by the Germans, combined with the garrulousness of the American military attaché in Cairo (one Col. Bonner Fellers), gave the German General Rommel a hidden edge in the desert war in North Africa in 1943.

JAPAN

The Black Dragon Society, Kokuryukai, was the most prominent of the many secret societies that did most of Japan's spying in the early part of the 20th century, in place of formal government organizations. The name comes from the Chinese characters for the river Amur, in Manchuria, and signifies the society's first goal, to expel the Russians from Manchuria across the Amur.

Kempei Tai, the Japanese Military Police, was founded in 1881. Stronger than any conventional military police, it became Japan's internal secret service during World War II.

THE UNITED STATES OF AMERICA

The CIA, the Central Intelligence Agency, was established in 1947 by executive order to coordinate the different intelligence agencies of the United States and correlate the intelligence collected. Headed by the director, Central Intelligence, who sits on the National Security Council, the Central Intelligence Agency has gradually taken over more and more of both the information-gathering and covert-action activities of the United States government.

---

the Intelligence Service that is usally being referred to by the word "Mossad."

[7]   The others are the American CIA, the Russian KGB, and the British SIS.

The CIC is the Counterintelligence Corps of the United States Army.

The Defense Intelligence Agency, DIA, is the intelligence-gathering arm of the Defense Department.

The FBI, Federal Bureau of Investigation, is the principal investigative branch of the United States government. Besides being responsible for investigating interstate crime and specific crimes that have been designated by statute, such as kidnaping, the FBI is also the counterespionage arm of the government.

The NSA, National Security Agency, was founded in 1952 for the purpose of safeguarding American codes and intercepting and decrypting the codes and ciphers of other countries. It is aided by, and provides aid to, three military agencies: the Army Security Agency (ASA), the Navy Security Group (NSG), and the Air Force Security Service (AFSS).

The ONI is the Office of Naval Intelligence, the intelligence service of the United States Navy.

The OSS, the Office of Strategic Services, was the espionage and sabotage organization of the United States headed by William (Wild Bill) Donovan during World War Two. Most of its operations were aimed at occupied Europe. It was disbanded in 1945, and is generally considered the direct precursor to the CIA.

SIS, the Signal Intelligence Service, was the United States Army's codebreaking section, from 1930 until the 1950s, when its functions were taken over by NSA and ASA.

X-2 was the counterintelligence section of the OSS.

USSR

The KGB is the latest link in the chain of secret services that has guarded the Russian people since the days of the tsar. Probably the largest secret organization in the world in terms of manpower, it shares with the Gestapo the distinction of being a secret service with a uniform. Founded soon after the revolution on December 20, 1917, as the Cheka (Special Commission), it has been called, variously, the GPU, the OGPU, the NKVD, and the MVB, until it received its present designation of Komitet Gosudarstvennoy Bezopasnosti, the Committee for State Security. It has primary responsibility for intelligence and counterintelligence in the Soviet Union, and is considered an arm of the CPSU, the Communist Party of the Soviet Union. Much of its resources are traditionally aimed at its own people.

The GRU, Glavnoye Razvedyvatelnoye Upravleni, is the Soviet military intelligence organization.

The Ochrana was the secret police under the tsar. It was mainly an organ of oppression aimed against the Russian people.

AND

The Spanish Secret Service is called "Sesid." Under Franco the Spanish security service was the "Seguridad."

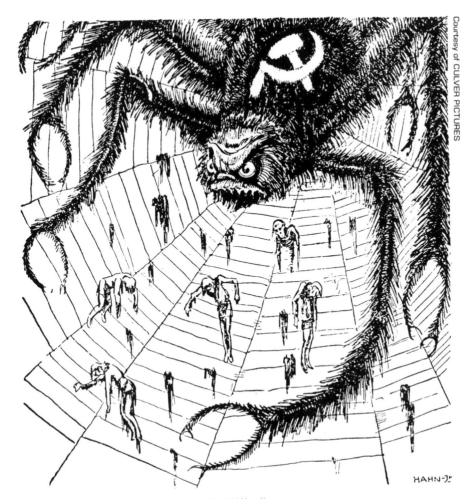

Courtesy of CULVER PICTURES

A European view of the NKVD before World War II.

The Portuguese security service, under Dr. Salazar, was the "Policia Internacional e de Defensa de Estato," or PIDE.

The Hanokmin (Hebrew for "avengers") was formed after World War II by former members of the Jewish Brigade of the British Army for the particular purpose of tracking down Nazi war criminals and those former SS men who had run the concentration camps.

The Irish Intelligence Service calls itself "G-2," while the Egyptian Intelligence Service calls itself "The Egyptian Intelligence Service," or EIS.

PART TWO: SOME ODD FACTS

A spy is eclectic; the more he knows, the more useful
he is. And the more a spy knows about the odd facts of espionage, the
more likely he or she is to keep out of trouble and stay alive.

In this section is a random compendium of interesting information
that will doubtless come in handy to you as Spymaster General. When
you least expect it, these tales and tidbits might even save your life. . . .

5 MICHMASH OR THE UTILITY OF HISTORY

The application of historical study is sometimes surprisingly direct. On February 14, 1918, the British 60th Division was preparing to attack the Turkish positions in Palestine, on the West Bank of the Jordan River. High on a rocky hill overlooking the attack route was the ancient village of Michmash, much the same then as it had been for the last 3,000 years. Except that now it was being held by a strong contingent of Turkish troops.

Michmash had to be taken, and quickly, or it could block the British advance.

A brigade was ordered to take the village, and the brigadier planned a frontal attack the next morning, up the rocky slope, in the face of the enemy. It would exact a heavy price in human lives, but it seemed the only way.

An officer in the attacking brigade, Major Vivian Gilbert, stayed awake that night trying to recapture a fleeting memory of the name—Michmash. It sounded biblical to him. He leafed through his bible and found the reference he remembered in 1 Samuel, chapters 13 and 14. As the King James Version has it:

> And the Philistines gathered themselves together to fight with Israel, thirty thousand horsemen, and people as the sand which is on the sea shore in multitude: and they came up, and pitched in Mich-mash, eastward from Beth-a-ven.

He read on, and what he read so intrigued him that he went to his brigadier's tent and woke him up. "Listen to this, sir," he said:

> Now it came to pass upon a day, that Jonathan the son of Saul said onto the young man that bare his armour, Come, and let us go over to the Philistines' garrison, that is on the other side. . .
>
> And between the passages, by which Jonathan sought to go over unto the Philistines' garrison, there was a sharp rock on the one side, and a sharp rock on the other side: and the name of the one was Bo-zez, and the name of the other Sen-eh.

> *The forefront of the one was situate northward over against Mich-*
> *mash, and the other southward over against Gib-e-ah. . .*
> *And both of them discovered themselves unto the garrison of the*
> *Philistines . . .*

The brigadier sat up and put on his jacket. "Very little has changed in Palestine throughout the centuries," he said, thoughtfully.

Major Gilbert read him the rest of the verses.

> *. . . And Jonathan said unto his armourbearer, Come up after me: for*
> *the Lord hath delivered them into the hand of Israel.*
> *And Jonathan climbed up upon his hands and upon his feet and his*
> *armourbearer after him: and they fell before Jonathan; and his*
> *armourbearer slew after him.*
> *And that first slaughter, which Jonathan and his armourbearer*
> *made, was about twenty men, within as it were an half acre of land,*
> *which a yoke of oxen might plow.*

And the Bible went on to describe that, while Jonathan attacked from the rear, Saul attacked from the front, "*and there was a very great discomfiture*" among the Philistines, who thought they were surrounded by a much larger force.

The brigadier ordered scouts sent out to check the accuracy of the biblical description. They reported that the passages mentioned in the Bible were still there, sharp rocks, plowable half-acre and all.

If Jonathan could surprise the Philistines, the brigadier decided, then his brigade could surprise the Turks by using the same passage.

One company was roused and sent in the dark to follow the route of Jonathan and his armourbearer, which they did, silently disposing of the few Turkish sentries they met. At dawn, they attacked.

The Turks, attacked by surprise and from the rear, fled down the hill they had been preparing to fight the British from—as the Philistines had done 30 centuries before.

And there was a very great discomfiture among the Turks. "We killed or captured every Turk that night in Michmash," Major Gilbert said afterward, "so that after thousands of years the tactics of Saul and Jonathan were repeated with success by a British force."

6 A TALE OF TWO SPIES

Tragedie is to seyn a certeyn storie,
As olde bokes maken us memorie,
Of him that stood in great prosperitie
And is y-fallen out of high degree
Into miserie and endeth wretchedly.

—*Geoffrey Chaucer*

This is the story of two men, the American General Benedict Arnold and the British Major John André. It is, in dramatic terms, a tragedy, the tale of a hero brought down by a fatal flaw in his own character.[1]

Benedict Arnold was not the first American traitor; a doctor named Benjamin Church has that distinction. But General Arnold was the most ambitious until the Walker family came along.

It was twisted ambition that drove Arnold into selling out his—I was going to say his "country," but the country didn't exist yet. And if Arnold's treachery had succeeded, it may well never have come into being.

Arnold began as a hero. Had he continued as he began, there would be statues of him in various public parks, and every town in America would have its Arnold Street. Colonel Arnold served in joint command with Ethan Allen as the Green Mountain Boys took Fort Ticonderoga.[2] He stood

---

[1]   Certainly for Arnold this is true. For André it is more a peripeteia.

[2]   "In the name of the Great Jehovah and the Continental Congress," as Allen put it.

Courtesy of The New-York Historical Society

Benedict Arnold

second-in-command to General Montgomery in a gallant and unsuccessful attempt to take Quebec City from the British, as they had taken it from the French 16 years before. Montgomery fell, and Arnold had his leg shattered by a bullet.

The attempt made him a popular hero,[3] and Congress made him a brigadier general. He then went on to defend Lake Champlain with a flotilla of hastily-made, poorly-armed galleys against a vastly superior British force. The British finally won, as vastly superior forces have a way of doing, but his spirited fighting cost them the summer.

Next he found himself fighting the British in Connecticut, where he had his horse shot out from under him and collected several musket-ball holes in his hat.

[3]   In England, too.

[4]   When the congressional accountants asked him for vouchers to back up his claims, he said his word of honor should be enough.

But if the British couldn't harm his body, the Continental Congress managed to wound his pride. They would not give him the seniority he thought he deserved, and they bickered with him on paying back some money he claimed to have expended.[4] Wounded pride can fester just as wounded flesh.

John André, a poet, musician, and artist of some ability, had purchased a commission in the British Army after his fiancée broke off their engagement. He had long dreamed of martial glory, but perhaps needed that impetus to push him into action. He found the reality differed from his imagination, at least in peacetime; his brother officers were mainly interested in whoring, gaming, and drinking.

In 1774 his regiment moved to Quebec. Before joining it he made a side trip to Philadelphia, at that time the most cosmopolitan of the Colonial cities. He found the City of Brotherly Love in a ferment, rife with anti-British sentiment.

André traveled in a leisurely fashion from Philadelphia to Quebec, keeping a journal full of sketches and comments on the interesting costumes and customs of the natives. It has been suggested that this was a spying expedition, but the British at that time were not interested in spying, feeling that the Colonial rabble would melt away at the first taste of grapeshot, and anyway no commander in his right mind would have chosen the aristocratic, bookish André as a spy.

When the Revolution started, and Montgomery took Montreal, André was captured with the rest of the British garrison and sent on parole back to Connecticut.[5] he was apparently harassed by some behind-the-lines heroes, who thought that picking on an unarmed British prisoner showed their manhood. He wasn't harmed, but it developed in him a distaste for the American rabble, whom he referred to as "peasants," and a feeling that it would be a good thing if the British beat them down. For the first time he was taking the war seriously.

André benefited from a general prisoner exchange and joined General Howe's troops in New York City. He spent a quiet and unwarlike winter on Staten Island, flirting with the local beauties and writing poetry.

Arnold, in the meantime, was getting increasingly unhappy with the Congress. He had gone into battle again, and again performed heroically, but other officers were getting posted senior to him. Why wouldn't Congress promote him? Because he had asked for it. To accede to his request, as one congressman explained to the disgust of a Virginia legislator who recorded it in his journal, "would be derogatory to the honor of Congress."

The fortunes of war now returned Major André to Philadelphia. In between riding out to fight the Rebels and being shot at from behind trees, walls, fences, rocks, and barns, André and the other young British officers amused themselves by arranging balls, to which they escorted the young

---

[5] That is, he promised not to fight again until he could be exchanged for an American prisoner, and the American officers believed him and sent him off on his own until such a thing could be arranged.

ladies of Philadelphia society. One of these young ladies was an 18-year-old named Peggy Shippen, daughter of a merchant whose neutrality in the war had a decidedly Tory[6] slant. Peggy herself was much more impressed by these well-dressed, elegant British officers than she had been by the ragged Rebel troops she had been surrounded by earlier. It is certain that Peggy and the major met, probable that they kissed, but it is not known just how intimate the relationship was. That doesn't matter. For the purposes of this story it is enough that they met, and of that there is no doubt.

Time passed. It was now 1778, and the British had left Philadelphia. George Washington appointed Benedict Arnold, who was recuperating from another wound in the leg, as the military commander of Philadelphia, and Arnold established his headquarters in a fine mansion whose Tory owners had left for more congenial parts. Arnold began using his position as military governor to make a lot of money for himself in ways that stretched the bounds of the acceptable. Little things that he wouldn't want talked about, like letting ships full of goods pass through the lines in return for a substantial piece of the profit. Perhaps he felt that, as he had spent a lot of his own money in the American cause—on such things as paying troops overdue wages so they wouldn't desert—he was entitled to it. If the Continental Congress wouldn't reimburse him, he would manage the job himself.

When the middle-aged Arnold (he was 36 at the time) began paying court to the lovely Peggy Shippen, her family was at first seriously annoyed. A Rebel officer, of whatever rank, was not a good catch for the daughter of a wealthy Tory merchant. But Peggy was a young lady who was used to having her own way, and she wanted Arnold. On the eighth of April, 1779, the loving couple were married.

Now Arnold's misdeeds were threatening to catch up with him. A court of inquiry was to look into his financial peccadilloes, as well as several more serious, although less well founded, charges made by those jealous of his success. General Washington indefinitely postponed the court, feeling that Arnold could not be spared at the moment to answer what were probably baseless charges.[7] After all, there was a war going on. But the threat of court-martial was now hanging over Arnold's head, and only he knew how accurate the charges were.

It was about now that Arnold and his new wife began contemplating how enjoyable life would be on the British side of the fence. In this most fluid of wars, with former friends, and even brothers, facing each other across loaded guns, it was not unheard of for a man, even an officer, to change sides. Montgomery, who died in the siege of Quebec, had been a British officer. Peggy Shippen's brother had sworn allegiance to the British, only to recant at his father's insistence when he was captured by Colonial troops. Nothing serious had happened to him.[8]

---

6   Pro-British.

7   Arnold had faced similar accusations before, and always gotten clear of them. Malfeasance charges seem to have been as popular with the Colonials as malpractice charges are with modern Americans.

If Arnold had merely gone over to the British side, he would have been welcomed by the British, and despised by the Colonials. But merely as a turncoat, not a traitor. There is a difference. But that wasn't enough for Arnold; he wanted his new friends to respect him. He needed to bring them something that would win their respect. And besides, he wanted a large sum of money for changing sides.[9] But what to bring? And how to get in touch with the British without getting himself and Peggy hanged?

In April of 1779 General Clinton put Captain André in charge of the British Army's intelligence in the New York area. Shortly after André's appointment, Arnold called Joseph Stansbury in to see him, at Peggy's suggestion. Stansbury was a merchant with strong Tory sympathies, feelings that Peggy had been aware of from the days when she had visited his shop in the company of her British officer boyfriends.

"General Arnold communicated to me," Stansbury wrote much later, "under a solemn obligation of secrecy, his intention of offering his services to the commander in chief of the British forces in any way that would most effectively restore the former government and destroy the then usurped authority of Congress, either by immediately joining the British Army or cooperating on some concerted plan with Sir Henry Clinton [the British commander]."

Stansbury, a meek and timid man, went through the lines to New York, his heart pounding triple-time every step of the way. He had legitimate commercial business in New York, and he carried no incriminating papers, but he had no pass, and what if his explanation was not believed? When he arrived he confided in a friend, another staunch Tory, the Reverend Jonathan Odell. Together the two of them went to see Captain André with their story.

André consulted with General Clinton, and composed a reply to take back to Arnold. He suggested communicating in invisible ink between the lines of innocent letters written to a young lady in Philadelphia, and another in New York. Stansbury even more nervously took this message back to the general.

Arnold rejected the idea of involving innocent young ladies, and that idea was dropped. But the communications continued. Each side had a problem. André wanted something concrete from Arnold, some act that would establish his allegiance. He wanted Arnold, in other words, to prove his treachery. But he would not commit the British Crown to paying the remuneration that Arnold demanded until the action was performed. Arnold on his part was willing to attempt some tangible act, but wanted the assurance that he would be paid on the attempt—win, lose, or draw—and welcomed over to the British side.

André had the additional difficulty that he couldn't be sure he was really in communication with the famous American general. It could have been

---

8   He was pardoned because of his youth, an excuse not open to General Arnold.

9   In effect he wanted the British to recompense him for what he thought the Continental Congress owed him.

some sort of complex *ruse de guerre* designed to catch the British out.

In the meantime Arnold's court-martial was scheduled again, and then dropped again when a British move caused the officers convened to return to the front line. Arnold was not yet resolved on treachery, despite his letters to André, which were already enough to hang him if discovered. It is probable that if the court-martial had been held then, and decided in his favor, he would have resumed his place among the patriots and Arnold Street would intersect Washington Avenue in many an American town today.

Captain André was promoted to major and appointed to the post of deputy adjutant general on the staff of General Clinton. And the British force in New York boarded ship and went off to attack Charleston, South Carolina.

Finally, after much delay, General Benedict Arnold faced a court-martial. At last, he thought, he would be cleared of the accusations of those jealous pygmies that were ruining his reputation.

The accusations did not include treason; there was no suspicion as yet of that. Several serious accusations were dropped before the trial for lack of evidence. There were four charges, varied and hard to prove: that he had given a pass to a brig called the *Charming Nancy* to enrich himself (true, but unprovable), that he had taken advantage of the closure of shops by military order to speculate in goods (true, but they had the wrong evidence); that he had used public wagons to carry private goods (true, but it depended on whether he had issued an order or requested a favor—a matter of interpretation as there was nothing in writing); and that he had imposed menial duties on a militiaman (piddling, and nobody took it seriously, except the militiaman in question).

Arnold gave a spirited defense, touching on his military career—as one of the first and most able supporters of the new nation—and his honor. He fully expected acquittal.

The judges found him innocent of two counts and guilty of the other two: the *Charming Nancy* pass and the wagons. They were willing, they said, to believe the transgressions no more than bad judgment, but a man in Arnold's position should weigh his judgments more carefully. They sentenced him to receive an official reprimand from General Washington.

Arnold thought himself badly used. He was also going broke, and had to move into a smaller house owned by his father-in-law. Thoughts of treason filled his mind. He began secretly to move what transportable assets he had to a Tory merchant in New York for transport to London.

Arnold decided what his gift to the British must be: West Point. If the British could take the fort at West Point, they could control the Hudson River and split the Colonies in twain. And West Point would be the perfect command for General Washington to give to a man who, because of his wounds—honorable battlefield wounds—could not sit a horse long enough to be useful to an army in the field. He suggested it to the general. Washington promised to consider the idea.

Arnold resolved to get back in touch with the British. He didn't want to mention his West Point scheme until he succeeded in getting the command.

When he came over, he said, he could help in an attack on Boston, Philadelphia, or any other place.

Major André was still in Charleston with General Clinton. Wilhelm von Knyphausen, the general commanding the Hessian troops in New York, sent a reply. He offered a small sum of money, and included a dictionary to use as a code book. Arnold consummated his treachery with von Knyphausen. His next letter included information about 6,000 French troops that were shortly to land on Rhode Island for an invasion of Canada.

General Clinton and Major André sailed back into New York harbor just in time to get Arnold's reply. André got back in touch with Arnold, who had upped his monetary demands. Now he wanted 10,000 pounds in front, and an annual pension of 500 pounds additional. He also told André of his West Point scheme. His price for that was 20,000 pounds, but he promised to deliver the garrison with all its men and supplies intact.

For a while they bickered about the money. The British, to mollify Arnold without committing themselves to anything, assured him that, although they could not quote a price before seeing what would be delivered for it, he "would have no cause to complain." They wanted to arrange a face-to-face meeting, still not absolutely sure that they were really dealing with Major General Benedict Arnold.

On August 3, 1780, General Washington signed the order putting General Arnold in command of the garrison at West Point.

From reports by Arnold and other spies, it became clear to General Clinton that the French troops to be landed in Rhode Island were no longer scheduled to attack Canada. They were going to be part of a two-pronged attack on New York City: the French from the north and Washington's army from the south.

To succeed in this, it would be necessary for Washington to move up and concentrate his stores of cannon, shot, powder, and other military supplies. And the perfect place to do that would be the fortress at West Point.

If General Clinton timed things right, he could capture Washington's supplies, split the country in half, and then concentrate his forces against the French and destroy them, all in one fell swoop. And the traitorous General Arnold was now in command of West Point.

Had General Clinton succeeded he would have gone down in the history books as a master strategist, and we would all speak English today. And he came close. Were it not for a fool named Smith. . . .

The history books all accuse Benedict Arnold, at this point, of trying to weaken the garrison at West Point. The exact opposite is true; he was trying to strengthen it. The more supplies and men there were, the more Clinton would capture. It was the usual hesitation of the Continental Congress, and the inefficiency of the Colonial Army, that kept the fort in a general state of disrepair.

It was now essential for Arnold to meet with a representative of the British so that details could be worked out. Major André decided that he should go himself. It appealed to his sense of the romantic, and there seemed little danger. He would go secretly, but in full British uniform. Arnold could no doubt secure the meeting place. And as for getting there and returning, well, he faced the normal hazards of war, but at least in uniform he couldn't be accused of being a spy.

After one unsuccessful try, when Arnold's barge was chased away by a British gunboat, they set up another meeting. Clinton was now resolved to take West Point immediately, as the supposed French reinforcements were blockaded by the British navy in the port of Brest. There was no point in waiting.

André came up the Hudson in a British sloop named the *Vulture*, and Arnold sent a local named Smith to get him. Smith, who wasn't too bright, was not privy to Arnold's secrets. He didn't know who he was getting. He thought it was a Tory landowner who wanted to complain about some property. A perfectly possible happening; it was a strange war.

Arnold and Smith enlisted a reluctant pair of brothers named Cahoon to help Smith row out to the *Vulture* and pick up a passenger. Arnold would wait in Smith's house on shore.

The Cahoons "did not choose to go," as they told Arnold. He said they had to go "for the good of the country." Fine, they said, but in the morning—it was too late now. Smith gave the brothers a drink, which seems to have turned the trick, and they left with him to row out to the sloop. After waiting an hour, Arnold got impatient and rode down to the landing to await the boat.

Major André, with a long blue coat concealing his British uniform, climbed down into the rowboat. He told Smith he was the John Anderson who Smith had come to get. Smith opined that it didn't matter to him *who* got in the boat so long as someone did and they could row back.

Finally, Major General Benedict Arnold of the Continental Army, commandant of West Point, and Major John André of the British Army, adjutant general to General Clinton, met face to face. How each must have stared into the darkness of that moonless night to see what the other looked like.

They went off and sat down with their backs to fir trees, and discussed treason. Arnold wanted 10,000 pounds for delivering the fort. André was only empowered to offer 6,000. Arnold was firm. André was tactful. He promised to see what he could do about getting Clinton to raise the ante.[10]

Then there was the problem of exactly *how* to turn the fort over to the British. American discipline was not the same as British discipline. If an order didn't make sense to an American infantryman, he was liable to ignore it. So General Arnold would have to issue a series of seemingly sensible orders that would result in the comparatively bloodless surrender of the garrison. It was an interesting technical problem, and they chewed it over for several hours.

Finally dawn was approaching, and it was time for the conspirators to part. It was now that, unnoticed by those involved, the skein began to unravel.

Smith, who was annoyed at being cut out of these secret conversations,[11]

---

[10]   Or so Arnold was to claim later.

[11]   Remember, Smith thought they were discussing property, not treason.

came over to tell them that it would shortly be dawn. Arnold asked Smith to row "Mr. Anderson" back to the *Vulture*. Smith went back to the Cahoon brothers and relayed the request. They were too tired.

For some reason neither Arnold nor André argued the point. Instead they rode back to Smith's house to spend the day. When Smith came upstairs with them and saw, for the first time, that his guest was in the uniform of a British major, he expressed surprise. Arnold explained that his friend, although merely a merchant, wore the uniform from "a sense of pride." Smith nodded, satisfied. But, as there were some less perceptive men who wouldn't understand, he thought that "Anderson" had better keep away from the window.

During the morning the *Vulture* had an artillery duel with a shore-based Colonial battery and retreated a few miles downstream, anchoring off Sing Sing to wait for the night so it could go back for André. The commander of the sloop was not going to chance losing General Clinton's favorite aide through any fault of his.

Arnold couldn't stay the day. He spent some time showing André some papers he had brought, gave him a couple to take back with him, which the major hid in his boot, and then left, heading for his barge to return to the fort. He left Smith with two passes, one to allow "Anderson" to return to New York by land, and the other by water. When he got back to the fort he took his wife aside and whispered the good news to her. In a few days West Point would belong to the British and 10,000 pounds would belong to the Arnolds.

Smith decided that he didn't want to row back out to the *Vulture*, and so he informed Major André that it was too dangerous, and that the Cahoon brothers wouldn't go.[12] He would accompany "Mr. Anderson" across the ferry, and get him well and truly started back to New York City, but "Mr. Anderson" would have to get rid of that British uniform.

André argued as best he could, but since he couldn't tell Smith that the reason he was wearing a British officer's uniform was because he *was* a British officer, he could make no headway against Smith's invincible ignorance. Smith loaned him a claret-colored coat with gold-laced buttonholes and a round hat. As the breeches and boots could pass for civilian, André kept those.

They started out toward the ferry, Smith in high spirits—he was on a secret mission!—and André in mortal fear that his moronic companion was going to give everything away. Smith insisted on engaging in conversation with every Rebel officer they passed, and whispering that he was on important business for General Arnold. Luckily none of them paid him any attention. Presumably they knew him.

Once across the ferry, with the onset of night, the road cleared out. They went on for some distance without meeting anyone, but finally ran into a Rebel sentry. Smith convinced the Rebel captain that they were on urgent

---

[12]   He didn't bother asking them.

Courtesy of CULVER PICTURES

The capture of Major André.

business for General Arnold, but the captain advised them to stop for the night. There were cowboys[13] in the area, he told them.

They spent the night in a local farmhouse, and continued early the next morning. After a few miles Smith turned back, saying they were too close to the British lines now for him to continue. André tried to conceal his delight.

He was near Tarrytown, which was considered British territory, when he was stopped by three ragged men who pointed muskets at him. One of them, a giant of a man, grabbed his reins. André told them that he was delighted to see them, as he was a British officer. That seemed to get a bad reaction, so he quickly switched his story, claiming to be on orders from General Arnold. He pulled out his pass.

"You said you was a British officer," the giant said, seeming unimpressed by the document. He could read, but it wasn't his strong point. "Where's your money?"

"Gentlemen, I have none," André replied. As, indeed, was true.

"A British officer and no money? Let's search him!" They dragged André off his horse and stripped him, searching for money. What they found instead were the papers he had hidden in his boot.

The giant struggled through the documents, and decided that they had caught them a spy. As they seemed overly interested in money, André tried to bribe them, saying that if they delivered him to the British lines he would see that they were rewarded.

---

13   The term was used for pro-Tory bandits, with the emphasis on "bandits," who roamed the no-man's land between the two armies. The Rebel version were called "skinners."

"If we deliver you to British lines," one of them replied, "you'll see that we are arrested."

André offered to let two of them keep him there, while the third took a note that would arrange for an exchange of their prisoner for a large sum of money. This they talked over for a long time, but they finally decided that it was a trick.

They delivered André to Colonel Jameson, in charge of the American outpost at North Castle. André, maintaining his poise, produced General Arnold's pass and insisted on being let through the lines.

But to Colonel Jameson the papers in "Anderson's" boot seemed to contain secret information about West Point, and they looked to be in the same handwriting as the pass. Even so, had he any right to disobey the written order of his superior officer? He sent André into another room while he thought it over. Finally he decided that, rather than send André on, he would send him back to General Arnold.

This cheered André up considerably. They'd just have to start all over again. Perhaps he could make it back to the *Vulture* this time.

Now things get confusing. Colonel Jameson decided to call André back, using the excuse that there were British troops spotted on the road. But he felt that he had to notify General Arnold, and so he sent a man to do so. But at the same time he sent another man, with the papers from André's boot, to General Washington, who was, curiously enough, en route to West Point. André was locked up in South Salem, waiting clarification of his identity. Arnold was having breakfast when an aide announced that General Washington would be there directly, and a dusty lieutenant named Allen handed him a letter from Colonel Jameson. Arnold ripped open the letter:

> *I have sent Lieutenant Allen with a certain John Anderson taken going to New York. He had a passport signed in your name. He had a parcel of papers taken from under his stockings, which I think of a very dangerous tendency. The papers I have sent to General Washington.*

A second letter explained that Mr. Anderson had been returned to custody.

Arnold told Lieutenant Allen to wait for an answer, and then hurriedly left. He took his barge to Stony Point, imagining that General Washington would start the hue and cry any second. The *Vulture* was waiting off Stony Point, and Arnold had his bargemen row him to her.

Now the British had Arnold, and the Americans had André. Which pleased nobody. "Arnold has betrayed us!" Washington exclaimed when he read the documents found in Major André's boot. "Whom can we trust now?"

Peggy Arnold threw a fit in her bedroom. She writhed about and screamed, "He is gone forever—there, there, there—the spirits have carried him up there! They have put hot irons on his head!" They called a doctor, and decided that the poor girl had gone temporarily mad when she heard about her husband's treason. It never occurred to anybody that she was in it with him. They sent her to join her father.

Arnold sent a letter to Washington from the *Vulture*. In it he tried to justify his treason, but succeeded only in rambling on about his grievances. He included a letter to his wife, but we don't know what was in that as Washington and his aides were too polite to read it, sending it up to Peggy Arnold unopened.

For a couple of days the British weren't sure what had happened to André. General Clinton finally realized that the Americans must have him, and set about wondering which of his Rebel prisoners he could exchange for the major. He gladly would have exchanged a dozen—nay, a hundred, for this talented, capable adjutant who had become a close friend.

But the American general orders announcing his capture called him a spy. How could that be?

André was captured behind enemy lines, out of uniform, with incriminating documents stuffed in his boot. The documents had been Arnold's idea, the civilian jacket Smith's, but no matter. He would be tried by court-martial as a spy.

Arnold was now safe among the British, resolved to do his best for their cause. He was convinced that, when his defection became common knowledge, Rebel troops would follow him by the score, by the hundreds, to the British side. But through a feeling that he had let André down, and perhaps a natural dislike of traitors, the British treated him with scorn. And the expected avalanche of deserters never came.

André was now jailed and about to face a court-martial. The records show that he behaved with courage, wit, and fortitude, and his American captors treated him with kindness and admiration. Technically he was a spy, but it was clear that it was mostly bad luck that had brought him to this pass.

Five days after he was captured, Major André was put on trial. The officers of the court found him guilty from his own statements, without having to call any other witnesses. He was sentenced to death.[14]

André asked if he might write General Clinton, and was given permission. His concern seems to have been to reassure Clinton that it wasn't the general's fault that he was captured:

> *I wish to remove from your breast any suspicion that I could imagine I was bound by Your Excellency's orders to expose myself to what has happened. The events of my coming within an enemy's posts and of changing my dress, which led me to my present situation, were contrary to my own intentions, as they were to your orders, and the circuitous route which I took to return was imposed (perhaps unavoidably) without alternative upon me.*

Colonel Aaron Ogden delivered Major André's letter to the British, along with a note from General Washington stating the court-martial verdict.

---

[14]   André asked to be shot like a soldier, if he must die, rather than being hanged like a spy. Washington's refusal has been misunderstood these many years. Had André been shot, that would have given fuel to possible British propaganda that the Rebels didn't really consider him a spy.

Self portrait of Major André, sketched with a pen on the day before his execution.

General Clinton was greatly upset. Colonel Ogden casually mentioned to one of the general's aides, while he was waiting, that if Clinton could somehow manage to let Arnold slip back into American hands, André could be saved from the gallows. This was all unofficial, as it was the sort of thing that couldn't be written down, but when the aide reported it to Clinton he had no doubt that it was true.

Clinton was tempted—is there no stronger word? and he would have liked nothing better than to have traded Arnold for André. But had he done so, no Rebel of whatever rank would ever desert again.

Two days later Major John André was hanged by the neck until he was dead.[15] No one in the American camp was happy about executing this likable young man, but it had to be done. The depths of Arnold's treason had

---

[15]   When he saw that he was to be hanged, André said, "I am reconciled to my fate, but not to the mode." Colonel Scammell read the death sentence, concluding with, "if you have anything to say, you can speak, for you have but a short time to live."

   "I have nothing to say, gentlemen, but this: you all bear witness that I meet my fate as a brave man."

decreed that someone must pay, and Arnold was out of reach. If the army seemed to treat this lightly, if Washington appeared not to care about treason, then the slender edifice might tremble, and collapse. "While we yielded to the necessity of rigor," Washington wrote, "we could not but lament it."

Arnold received a commission as colonel in the British army. He did nothing of note. Eventually Peggy joined him, and they went to live in London. He was surprised that the British seemed to regard him with distaste. He tried various ventures, but without exception they failed; and he had neither friends nor money. On June 14, 1801, he died.

A memorial to Major John André was raised in Westminster Abbey, final resting place of Britain's heroes.

Years later, after both Benedict and Peggy Arnold were dead, Aaron Burr told a story. When Peggy Arnold was being driven to her father's, after her husband had fled to the *Vulture*, they had stopped for the night at the house of Theodora Provost, the widow of a British officer.[16] The sick, upset Peggy retired to an upstairs bedroom, and Mrs. Provost came up to see after her.

Peggy, feeling safe in the bedroom of a British officer's widow, confessed to Mrs. Provost. The hysterics, she revealed, were phony, and she was "heartily sick" of them. Far from being upset at her husband's actions, she had urged them on him. It had taken "great persuasion and unceasing perseverance" to convince Major General Benedict Arnold to connive at treason.

But Peggy Shippen always got what she wanted.

---

[16]   Burr got the story from Theodora, whom he married after the war.

7 THEY ALSO SPIED

As spymaster general, you will find the people you need come from a wide variety of civilian ranks. Don't hesitate to use a promising agent because he's a novelist or she's an exotic dancer.

Many people have engaged in intelligence work of one sort or another at one time in their lives, coming from and moving on to some entirely different field in which they then gained prominence. Here is a list of just a few of the names I've run across that might be of interest:

Pierre Augustin Caron de Beaumarchais, 18th-century playwright, author of *The Barber of Seville* and *The Marriage of Figaro*, son of a watchmaker who followed in his father's profession long enough to become *horloger du roi*,[1] before abandoning it for more exciting pursuits; went to London several times as a secret agent for Louis XVI.

Moe Berg, star catcher for the Boston Red Sox and the Washington Senators in the 1930s, was in the OSS during World War II.

Daniel Defoe, author of *Robinson Crusoe* and *Moll Flanders*, was, at the start of the 18th century, a secret agent for the government of Queen Anne.

Douglas Fairbanks, Jr., was a member of the SOE, the Special Operations Executive, and spent much of World War II on a sailboat in the Mediterranean, picking up and delivering spies.

Ian Fleming, creator of James Bond, was in British Intelligence during World War II.

John Ford, Hollywood director of such films as *Stagecoach*, *The Grapes of Wrath*, and *Tobacco Road*, served in the OSS during World War II.

Graham Greene, British novelist, author of *Our Man in Havana*, *The Third Man*, and many other works, was head of station in West Africa for SIS[2] during World War II.

W. Somerset Maugham, British novelist, author of *The Razor's Edge* and *Of Human Bondage*, among many other notable works, was a secret agent

---

[1]   Watchmaker to the king.

[2]   The British intelligence service, also known as MI.6.

for the British in Europe during World War I. He recounted his experiences in fictional form in the novel *Ashenden*.

Christopher Marlowe, Elizabethan playwright, whose genius has been compared to that of Shakespeare, but who died too young for it to flower fully,[3] is believed to have done espionage work in Europe for Sir Francis Walsingham, Elizabeth's spymaster.

Jasper Maskelyne, a British stage magician, the fourth generation in a famous family of magicians, used his expertise in illusion to fool the forces of General Rommel in the deserts of North Africa as to the location and strength of the British forces. He also designed special equipment for espionage and POW escape efforts.

Paul Morphy, who was the world chess champion from 1858 to 1862, was a spy for the Confederacy during the Civil War. It is perhaps worth noting that, when he proposed marriage to a young lady in his home town of New Orleans, she replied that her father would never let her wed a "mere chess player."

Courtesy of the New York Public Library Collection

Timothy Webster, chief spy of the Pinkerton Secret Service in the Civil War.

---

[3]   He died at the age of 29 in a tavern brawl. See p. 85.

Alan Pinkerton, founder of the Pinkerton Detective Agency, served as a spy for the North during the Civil War, and later organized and ran Lincoln's counterespionage service.

Count Rumford, the British physicist and statesman, as Major Benjamin Thompson of the New Hampshire Militia, was a spy for the British during the American Revolution.

Courtesy of the New York Public Library

Benjamin Thompson, Count Rumford.

Joseph Stalin (Iosif Vissarionovich Dzhugashvili), effectively dictator of the U.S.S.R for 30 years until his death in 1953, was a spy and an agent provocateur for the *Ochrana*, the Tsar's secret police, before the revolution.

Alan Turing, who was responsible for much of the intellectual speculation leading to the computer, was the genius behind the development of Ultra, the secret device that broke the German Enigma code machines during WWII.

Alice Marble, four times United States women's singles tennis champion (1936, 1938-40), answered the call of her country and went to Switzerland in the last days of the Third Reich to spy out the Swiss banking records the Nazis kept with Marble's pre-war flame, Hans Steinmetz.

WHAT IS A SPY?

The author served as a spy for the British in occupied Belgium during World War One.

In novel and film we see the spy pictured as a brilliant society woman or a celebrated dancer or a diabolically clever vamp luring to her perfumed boudoir the general of the opposing army and thus securing a complete outline, with sketch map, of forthcoming military operations. The Spies I Knew were not at all like that. They were friends and neighbors of mine, simple folk who burned with one idea, to obstruct, hamper and if possible turn back the brutal invader of their country.

The type of spy who disgraces the world by selling his own country's secrets is never satisfactory even to his employers, for if he is a traitor to his own people he will more than likely betray also those who employ him.

The type whose aim is personal gain, even though no thought of treachery is present, is equally unsatisfactory, for there is always the danger that he will succumb to temptation and sell out to the highest bidder.

The type actuated by a sense of burning wrong, fancied or real, is likewise dangerous. His reports are generally biased and sometimes ridiculously distorted. His intense desire for revenge warps his judgment beyond his own control.

Desired above all is the spy constantly drawn on by deep patriotic motives. He may be a good hater, for it savors of sophistry to pretend that one can love one's own country deeply without hating those who maltreat it, but he must be rational and cool.

Three rules about spying we all learned early in the war:

(1)   Knowledge of our activities must be held within the smallest possible circle. For a long time only my mother and Alphonse the Alsatian knew that I was the mythical "Laura," and not at any time did more than five other persons know that I was a spy. In turn, I knew positively of only five fellow workers though of course I was aware that there existed hundreds of others in the occupied area.

(2)   A spy must never seem clever. The British Intelligence Service went to great lengths to establish its own stupidity in German eyes, thus gaining the inestimable advantage of being underrated by the opposing organization. One of the secrets of Canteen Ma's phenomenal success was the belief, carefully fostered by herself, that she could neither read nor write.

(3)   The *obvious* is the safest. Very early in the war we discarded most of the conventional "tricks," such as specially thin parchment paper, invisible ink, code messages and secret pockets in our clothing. These things the opponent expects and looks for. I used to write my messages in ordinary language on ordinary note paper with no attempt whatever to disguise my handwriting, merely signing them "Laura." I tried always to seem open, guileless and, above all, inconspicuous.

—From *Spies I Knew*
by Marthe McKenna

8 IF YOU SEE ANYTHING . . .

From shortly before the First World War to shortly before the Second World War the spy novel was very popular in France. On every tobacconist's newsstand there were dozens of cheap paperback spy novels.

Additionally, in the 1920s, spy films came into vogue in France, and hundreds were made over the next dozen years.

A substantial number of these novels and movies, were commissioned by the officers of the French Deuxième Bureau.

Were they, perhaps, embarrassed by the low literary standards of the French spy novel, or by the inaccuracies of the spy movies, and doing their bit to improve the breed? *Mais, non,* their aims were more subtle than that.

In each of these *oeuvres* there would somewhere be a scene where the dashing young Deuxième Bureau officer would shake hands with the earnest innocent civilian. "If you see anything suspicious," the dashing young officer would say, "sit down immediately and write a note to Monsieur le Chef, Deuxième Bureau, Paris. That will be sufficient address."

The novels and films were financed in the hope that this one scene, buried amid the otherwise ridiculous plot, would remain with the citizen-reader. That if he[1] by some chance *did* see anything suspicious, he would indeed drop a note to M. le Chef.

I have not seen any record of the results of this attempt to alert the public by such novel means, except that the books and films were a vast financial flop. Government, even in its secret branches, has never managed to make a profit in any artistic endeavor. *Quelle domage.*

---

[1]   I'm not being chauvinistic (even though it is a French word). The readers, as with other sorts of French novels, were overwhelmingly male.

NEUTRALS

Portugal was neutral, and so to Portugal came the agents official and unofficial of many countries and countries on both sides. It was not possible to learn in Berlin what was happening in London, but it might well be possible to hear, or guess, or deduce in neutral Portugal what was happening in both. And further, it might be possible to spread information (and make it appear credible) of what was *not* happening in London or Berlin and yet have it believed in the other place. And so Lisbon became a kind of international clearing-ground, a busy ant-heap of spies and agents, where political and military secrets and information—true and false, but mainly false—were bought and sold and where men's brains were pitted against each other. There was, of course, more in it than this. The life of the secret agent is dangerous enough, but the life of the double agent is infinitely more precarious. If anyone balances on a swinging tight-rope it is he, and a single slip must send him crashing to destruction.

—John Masterman
The Case of the Four Friends

(Sir John Masterman was the head of the Twenty Committee, the section of the British counterintelligence service that ran double agents during World War Two. The Case of the Four Friends is a novel, but certainly based upon experience.)

9 AT THE MOVIES

Spy novels and films have had as much effect on the reality as the reality has had on the fiction. Before World War I, Kaiser Wilhelm was convinced of the invincibility of the British Secret Service (at the time practically nonexistent) by the novels of E. Phillips Oppenheim. All of Europe suffered from spy jitters in the '30s, enhanced by the novels of John Buchan. Hitchcock's 1935 film of the Buchan novel, *The Thirty-Nine Steps*, uses the espionage background to explore Hitchcock's favorite theme of the naive man caught up in events beyond his control.

The 1936 Hitchcock film, *Secret Agent*, is based upon a play by Campbell Dixon, which is based on the novel *Ashenden*, by W. Somerset Maugham, which in turn is based upon Maugham's real experiences as a British agent during the First World War. Each layer of change separated fact from fiction a little more, but it is a good story, well told.

Courtesy of CULVER PICTURES

Garbo as the enticing Mata Hari.

Mata Hari became instantly immortal with her execution at the hands of the French during World War I (see chapter 13). Although she probably never was a spy, and certainly lacked many of the qualities of the successful exotic dancer or courtesan, history will ever use her name as a synonym for all three.

In this 1932 film, which had as little to do with reality as such things usually do, Greta Garbo played the spy (seen here with Lionel Barrymore), and did an exotic dance number that is highly regarded among connoisseurs of such things.

In the 1952 film, 5 *Fingers*, based on a true incident, James Mason portrayed "Cicero," the German code name for the agent who appeared at their embassy in Ankara one day during World War II, and offered to sell them secret Allied documents. When the film was made the identity of "Cicero" was not known, but 10 years later, in 1962, an Albanian named Elyesa Bazna wrote a book revealing that he, while the valet of the British

James Mason in *5 Fingers*.

Ambassador in Istanbul,[1] had photocopied every secret document passing through the embassy safe. There is still a dispute as to whether "Cicero" was merely a German agent, or was a double agent, secretly working for the British MI.5. Bazna sued the peacetime German government because their Nazi predecessors had paid him in counterfeit U.S. currency. He lost.

---

[1]   Sir Hugh Knatchbull-Hugessen, a man not noted for great care or good security.

A scene before the lady vanishes.

Dame May Whitty, as the lady who vanishes in *The Lady Vanishes*, is that most wonderful of God's creatures, an elderly spinster secret agent (seen here with Margaret Lockwood). This 1938 Hitchcock film is based on the book, *The Wheel Spins*, by Ethel Lina White.

Fräulein Doktor?

Dino DeLaurentiis's 1968 film version of *Fraülein Doktor* and her spy school is one that the serious-minded Elsbeth Schragmüller (see chapter 15) might not recognize. As you can see by the photograph (where Suzy Kendall, at left, has found out what interests scientist Capucine), it is recommended to all serious students of—er—espionage.

PART THREE: SPIES, SPYMASTERS & THE LESSONS OF HISTORY

"If the Pharaoh Memptah had been given an efficient intelligence service, there would have been no Exodus."

—*Sir Basil Thompson.*

It was once said by a gentleman named Santayana that anyone who doesn't study history is doomed to repeat it. This admonition is generally ignored today, probably because, as it was said more than five years ago, nobody today has ever heard of it.

We live in an age where the words "once upon a time," are applied to anything that happened before last Thursday. And, as with most fables, historical narratives are regarded with amusement and the narrators with suspicion. As a result, we are busy repeating a lot of history. Mostly the bad parts.

To help you with your heavy responsibilities as spymaster-general of Freedonia, here are some stories of an assortment of spies and spymasters of yesteryear, good, bad, and indifferent, and how they fared. These stories will serve as object lessons, as moral fables, and as a certain amount of history that you won't have to repeat.[1]

---

[1]   For an example of the advantage of a thorough knowledge of history, see chapter 5, "Michmash."

10 SIR FRANCIS WALSINGHAM

Elizabeth I of England was a Protestant queen. Her older half-sister, Queen Mary, had been a Catholic, and what is more had wedded His Most Catholic Majesty, Philip II of Spain. Had Mary not died young[1], had she succeeded in having a child—preferably a boy child—then you and I would probably speak Spanish today.

Philip II had managed to convince himself that he had a holy mission to convert England back to Catholicism. While Mary lived he had instituted a reign of terror in Protestant England, and he was loath to give it up.

Elizabeth was much more tolerant of the Catholics than her sister had been of the Protestants, but this wasn't nearly enough to satisfy Philip. He didn't want Catholicism to be tolerated in England, he wanted it to be mandatory. His troops were busy in the Netherlands, doing their best to stamp out Protestantism root and branch, and it galled him to see it flourishing right across the channel.

And Spain was the great power of the age. In a contest between England and Spain, nobody in his right mind would have wagered a ducat on England.

---

[1] She was 43 when she died, but she reigned for only five years.

This was but one of the troubles facing the 25-year-old Elizabeth when she ascended the throne. England had just lost Calais to the French, who didn't seem to think that was enough. The Dauphin Francis, heir to the throne of France, was married to Mary Stuart, "Queen of Scots," who, as the great-granddaughter of Henry VII, had a plausible claim on the throne of England. Francis and Mary had already started calling themselves king and queen of England from the safety of the French court. Soon Mary was to land in Scotland and try her luck from the north.

Pope Pius, under the prodding of Philip of Spain, declared that Elizabeth was a heretic, and it was the duty of every good Catholic to see that her reign was as short as possible. Jesuit priests were landing in England to find out just how much trouble it would be to assassinate the Protestant queen.

Elizabeth needed advisors she could trust. But more, the advisors needed to know what was happening in Spain, in France, in the Vatican, in Scotland, and in England itself, to make rational decisions and give useful advice.

Certain ages, certain times, certain places, perhaps certain people, seem to provoke greatness. Perhaps it is carried in the genes, and rises of itself every so many generations, or perhaps it is latent and needs but some spark to set it off. Nonetheless it seems that in some fortunate times and places greatness is in the very air. Periclean Athens was such a place, as were Republican Rome, Renaissance Italy, and Revolutionary America.

And the England of Elizabeth, at the time of its greatest need for almost the next 400 years, produced such people as the world has seldom seen—Marlowe, Shakespeare, Francis Bacon, Frobisher, Francis Drake, Lord Cecil, Lord Essex, and not the least Elizabeth herself, who kept her head, her throne, and her kingdom, and gained the grudging respect of every other monarch in Europe—and the love of her own people.

The first three of these she owed in large measure to the ability and loyalty of her secretary of state and spymaster, Sir Francis Walsingham.

It could be said that Walsingham invented the secret service; surely he developed the use of espionage as an instrument of national will, rather than an enlargement of his own power. He used it from first to last to further the Queen's policies, and not his own, and to meet England's needs, and not his own—even while he was paying for it largely out of his own pocket because the parsimonious Elizabeth could not be cozened out of another penny, not even to save her life.

And save her life it did, time after time, uncovering plots by disguised Jesuit priests, disaffected Catholic nobles, and disingenuous courtiers secretly working for the exiled Mary, Queen of Scots.[2]

Walsingham made good use of college students, who at the time were expected to travel around Europe as a part of their education. Many of them settled in Italy for a time (the British have always had an affinity for settling

---

[2]   Some people suspect that some of the plots were not as serious as Walsingham made them out to be, that he created plots where there was only tenuous evidence in order to get more money out of the queen. That may be, but many of the plots were very real, and the money was always very short.

in Italy for a time). Walsingham put the more useful ones on salary—not a large salary, the pay of an intelligence agent has never been more than adequate—and put them to hearing what they could hear. It is believed that one of his agents was a Cambridge student named Christopher Marlowe, who went on to rival Shakespeare as a creator of Elizabethan drama, until his mysterious death in a tavern brawl at the age of 29.[3]

Walsingham's agents intercepted and decoded messages smuggled to Mary, Queen of Scots, in kegs of beer. They discovered and exposed the plots of Babington, Throgmorton, and others against the life of their queen; they kept tabs on the French spies that came to England in boat after boat; and they kept an eagle eye on Philip of Spain. Perhaps their greatest coup was in March of 1587, when they handed to Walsingham, to pass on to Her Majesty, an exact copy of the report of the marquis of Santa Cruz, grand admiral of the Spanish navy, to His Most Catholic Majesty Philip II, on the state of readiness of the Grand Armada being gathered to invade England. A fully detailed report, it listed the ships, stores, equipment, and men being gathered to do what Philip thought was God's work, and the condition of each.

The strength of Walsingham's agents lay in the fact that they were, first and foremost, Englishmen, and subjects of Elizabeth, whom they loved and respected. Some of them actually were Catholics, who didn't think that religion gave the Spanish king the right to murder their queen—even if she were a Protestant. Some of them were willing to be Catholics for a while, some were willing to be called Catholics, and some probably just avoided the subject, but they knew where their allegiance lay. And it was with their sceptered isle and its Faery Queen, its Virgin Queen, not with pouting Philip or plotting Pius.

The rest of Europe at this time, especially the gentry and the nobility, felt no allegiance to any country. They might swear fealty to a king, a duke, or a pope, but it was to his person, not his land. But the stirrings of nationalism were growing in the Netherlands, where the stubborn Dutch were fighting Philip's deputy, the duke of Alva, for the right to be Dutch, and in England, which had a queen who declared to Parliament that "Nothing, no worldly good under the sun, is so dear to me as the love and good-will of my subjects."

Thus Walsingham, the founder of a national secret service, had not only a queen, but a nation, to serve and to save. He served both faithfully until his death, and he went through his entire fortune in supporting his nation's secret service when Elizabeth would not allocate the monies he thought necessary.

---

[3]   Some believe that he was murdered by the secret service—or the Spanish—because he knew too much. Others think that his death was staged by the secret service to get him out of the country. Of these latter, a smaller subset further believe that he snuck back into the country to write "Shakespeare's" plays.

THE CHEVALIER D'ÉON

Charles Geneviève Louis Auguste André Timothée d'Éon de Beaumont is of the stuff that dreams—and books, and movies—are made. I call your attention to the lack of a hand of fiction over this section. The story you are about to read is historical fact, mostly verifiable, and the strangest parts are the most thoroughly verified.

Charles Geneviève Louis Auguste, a slender, delicate-looking child, was dressed in girl's clothes by his mother until he was seven years old. His school comrades in his home town of Tonnerre made the sort of fun of him that one would expect until, as a teenager, he discovered what he was good at: fencing. He also, apparently, excelled at the study of the law, taking his doctorate in civil and canonical law before he was 20; but it was his skill with the épée that gained him the respect of his contemporaries.

Chevalier d'Éon took to the bar in Tonnerre, but didn't practice very long. Louis XV called the young man to Paris and told him that he had need of a good lawyer who could fence: Would the chevalier be willing to undertake a secret mission for France?

It must have been one of the great moments of revelation, like Newton being hit with the apple or Darwin staring at a finch, when Charles Geneviève Louis Auguste André Timothée d'Éon de Beaumont, kneeling before his sovereign, suddenly realized what his role in life would be.

In 1755 a French secret agent named Chevalier Douglass was on his way to St. Petersburg to visit the tsarina Elizabeth Petrovna. Well, it wasn't as simple as that.

It goes like this:

George II, who was on the throne of England (Scotland, Wales, Ireland, etc., etc.), also held the Germanic state of Hanover (through his grandfather who had been the Elector of Hanover). Although he preferred England (Scotland, Wales, Ireland, etc., etc.), Hanover was, after all, his ancestral home. And George was afraid that France—or maybe Prussia—had covetous eyes on Hanover.

King George needed troops to defend his precious Hanover, and he believed in getting troops wherever he could. His British subjects wouldn't go and fight in Hanover—not a chance—but if he could find some poor peasants from some backward country and buy them cheap, well, that was different.[1]

Russia at the time was a huge but backward country, which didn't produce a surplus of anything but peasants. The Russian chancellor, Bestucheff, agreed to a treaty where Russia would send 30,000 men to the aid of Hanover, or wherever else King George decided he needed them, for a large lump of English gold—and a smaller lump wnich was to go directly into Bestucheff's copious pocket.

Louis XV, who didn't like the idea of 30,000 armed men, even if they were peasants, wandering around Europe at the behest of George II, knew that Chancellor Bestucheff could draw treaties, but that only the sovereign herself could sign them. He received word that the treaty had not yet been signed by the tsarina.[2] And there was a good chance that Louis, or his emissary, could talk her out of signing by offering those blandishments with which one monarch tempts another: friendship, money, help against the nobles.

The problem was that Louis couldn't get an emissary in to see Elizabeth Petrovna. The daughter of Peter the Great, and ruler of all the Russias since Tsar Ivan IV had been kicked out by the nobles, was practically a prisoner in her own palace. Chancellor Bestucheff, with the help of even more English gold, was keeping Her Imperial Majesty isolated from the influence of foreign opinion. His tools were flattery and licentious pleasure, and throwing night-long balls; the tsarina was particularly susceptible to flattery, and she loved to dance. The chevalier de Valcroissant had been tossed into prison and charged with being a spy for merely trying to tender his respects to the tsarina. The fact that he *was* a spy was not relevant.

---

[1]   His son, George III, had a similar policy in his American colonies, and fought his rebellious subjects with Hessian mercenaries, which even many British thought was a bit much.

[2]   In those days there was always a great time delay between drawing up a treaty and signing it. Copies had to be officially translated into the relevant languages—in this case, probably French and English, as French was the official court language of Russia—and then carried by hand back and forth between the two countries. It took months to get even the simplest agreement signed.

Chevalier Douglass, who claimed to be travelling *"for his health,"* met his niece, the lovely Lia de Beaumont, at Anhalt, and together the two of them continued their meandering way to St. Petersburg. His doctors, it seems, had ordered Chevalier Douglass to move to a cold climate.

Lia was a shy, demure young lady, *"small and slight, with a pink and white complexion and pleasing, gentle expression,"* as one admirer described her. Court artists found her beauty such that they had to record it, and several paintings and miniatures survive to this day to attest to their judgment. On the trip to Petersburg she carried a handsomely-bound copy of Montesquieu's *L'Esprit des Lois*, to read during the tedious journey.

When they arrived in Petersburg, Chevalier Douglass made the expected attempts to see the tsarina, and was easily blocked by the chancellor's agents. He didn't push the issue, since Russian prisons are noted for their unpleasantness.

Meanwhile the lovely Lia met and enchanted the vice-chancellor, a gospodyn named Woronzoff. The vice-chancellor was already well disposed toward France, and the allure of the charming and innocent Mademoiselle de Beaumont completely won him over.

Woronzoff presented Lia to Tsarina Elizabeth, who also was immediately enchanted. Mademoiselle Lia de Beaumont was young, lively, gay, and a source of gossip about the notorious court of Louis XV. What absolute monarch could have resisted?

Lia de Beaumont was made a maid of honor, and then a reader to the tsarina. It is probable that one of the first books she chose to read was *L'Esprit des Lois*, with emphasis on the elaborate binding. Carefully inserted there was a letter from Louis XV to Elizabeth, suggesting that the two rulers engage in a secret correspondence. And, just to keep it secret, Louis included a royal cipher for her majesty to use. The empress must have been impressed by Louis's concern, and by the bravery of the slender young girl who had smuggled the message to her.

"I regret to inform you," the British ambassador soon wrote to London, "that the Chancellor is finding it impossible to induce Her Majesty to put her signature to the Treaty which we so earnestly desire."

At some time the empress must have learned the truth—that the shy, delicate young mademoiselle was really a chevalier named d'Éon—and apparently she was not overly shocked. It is recorded that she offered him a title and a commission in her army. The chevalier declined, with thanks, and received instead a diamond-encrusted snuffbox as a memento.

To the end of his life d'Éon continued as a spy and master of intrigue, in both male and female attire, taking time out to serve with distinction in the army during several of Louis's numerous wars. He grew familiar with England while studying the fortifications of her channel counties, with an eye toward picking an invasion site if Louis should get peeved enough at George, and decided to retire to England when he fell out of favor with Madame Pompadour, who had considerable influence on Louis XV.

Louis sent messages entreating d'Éon to return to Paris, but d'Éon, well informed about what was happening and having an instinct about keeping his head out of the lion's mouth, refused. To further the indignity of refusing his sovereign, he demanded a pension be paid him there in England. When Louis hedged, d'Éon reminded him that he had letters which would be very embarrassing to the French monarch if released to the British public.

Louis, or one of his aides, hit upon the expedient of trying to prove that d'Éon was crazy, and getting him locked up in an asylum. They hired a chimney sweep to climb down d'Éon's chimney and make weird groaning sounds. The chevalier would report the noises, the authorities would investigate, and find nothing, and everyone would assume that d'Éon was insane. Upon which he would be repatriated to France as a madman. As simple as that.

Unfortunately the Chevalier d'Éon was not the sort to run screaming into the street when he heard strange noises in his chimney. Instead he took his sword and poked it up the chimney to see what would happen. There were a couple of even stranger noises, a scream or two, and the chimney sweep came tumbling down, and the true story came tumbling out.

The agents of Louis XV tried one or two more little tricks; they drugged him and were taking him off in a sedan chair when he came to and chased off his attackers. They sent a professional duelist to challenge him, and he frightened the professional off with a demonstration of his skills with both pistol and rapier. To encourage the notion that he should be left alone, d'Éon released one or two of the minor letters. They only created a small stir, but henceforth Louis ceased bothering him, realizing that release of the strongest of the letters would probably have led to war with England.

Sometime after that he actually went back to work for Louis, and returned most of the letters, holding back just one or two of the worst in case His Majesty once again had a change of heart.

D'Éon could never decide whether to dress as a man or a woman, and kept alternating throughout his life. Many believed that he *was* actually a woman, who liked the freedom she got in dressing and acting as a man. At the time England was in a betting fever. Large sums of money were wagered on the most inconsequential happenings; and one of the favorite bets was the true sex of the chevalier d'Éon. Half England bet one way, and half the other. Insurance policies were taken out on the result. One bettor sued another to collect; and thus a court decision depended upon d'Éon's true sex. But nobody could figure out a— ah—gentlemanly way to force him to reveal the truth.

He must have enjoyed the confusion. When he was 50 years old he put on his woman's garb and met and defeated in a fencing bout the chevalier St. George, a French champion, with the prince of Wales in the crowd watching.

When the French Revolution broke out, he offered to serve as a fighting man. When he was turned down, he tried to enter several convents where, "as a nun," he could end his days.

He was 80 years old when he died. The attending physician confirmed that he had been, indeed, a man. For 60 years no one had been sure.

He must have died laughing.

Courtesy of CULVER PICTURES

Mademoiselle de Beaumont or the Chevalier D'Éon

12 COLONEL ALFRED REDL

Football in Prague—Storm I. v. Union V. Score 5-7 (Halftime 3-3). Storm I. was the weaker team because of the absence of Wagner and Marck. Atja alone was not strong enough to withstand the opposition he had to face.

—Prager Tageblatt, Monday, 26 May, 1913

If Herr Wagner, the best locksmith in Prague, had not been an ardent football player, and if his team, Storm I, had not played Union V on Sunday, 25 May, 1913, and lost 7-5, then I should probably not be telling you this story; it would still be locked up in the secret archives of Imperial Austria, and not even the emperor himself would have known the whole of it.

In 1900 General Baron von Giesl, the head of the Austro-Hungarian Imperial Secret Service appointed Major Alfred Redl chief of the Kundschafts Stelle,[1] the counterintelligence bureau.[2] Redl brought along a keen intelligence, an inquiring mind, a liking for intrigue, and a fascination for modern gadgets. In a short time he had transformed the K.S. headquarters in Vienna into a museum of the latest techniques in counterespionage.

---

[1] Literally "Information Service."

[2] Which apparently had some intelligence functions also.

Major Redl's office was furnished like a luxurious living room, complete with soft furniture and expensive paintings on the walls. When a guest in whom Redl was interested entered the office he was offered a glass of a fine ancient Tokay, a cigarette, or possibly a candy if he didn't smoke, and some interesting, if meaningless, conversation. He could not fail to notice the pile of secret files neatly stacked on one corner of the desk.

At some point in the conversation, the phone would ring[3], and after a brief conversation Major Redl would excuse himself from the room to take care of some problem that couldn't wait. The guest, if he were a spy as Redl supposed, or even if he were merely possessed with normal curiosity, couldn't help being seized with an intense desire to look through the stack of secret files.

He would look around. The walls were solid, the doors were· solid, nobody hiding under the desk, the windows both looked out on the street. He would take a chance. Quickly he would riffle through the secret files until he found whichever one most interested him, say the one on Rumelia. Jogging the files at that point so that he could put the Rumelian file back in a moment, he would open it and read through the few pages as quickly as he could. He was not hurried.

When Redl returned, he would find the files stacked just as he had left them, and his guest perhaps immersed in a book of Persian poetry pulled from the shelves. Redl would apologize, refill his guest's glass from the age-encrusted Tokay bottle, and resume the conversation.

After the guest left the technicians would come in. They would lift the guest's fingerprints off the minium-coated[4] cigarette tray, or the minium-coated bonbon dish if the guest didn't smoke. They would take the plate film from the cameras concealed behind the paintings and get a full face and a profile photograph of the guest. They would remove the wax disk from the gramophone that had been recording the entire conversation.

Then they would remove the file of "secret" documents from the desk. By developing the light-sensitive chemicals impregnated in the paper, they could tell which document the guest had looked at longest, and therefore what subject or subjects he was most interested in.[5]

Major Redl originated many methods that are still in use by counter-espionage services and police departments today, including maintaining a file of fingerprints and photographs of everyone whom the dual empire might be remotely interested in. He wrote several books on the techniques of espionage which were used as bibles by the K.S., and were kept in manuscript only, as they were considered much too sensitive, too secret, to have printed.

In 1905 General Baron von Giesl, Major Redl's mentor, was put in command of the Eighth Corps, considered the most important corps in the

---

[3]   By means of a push button concealed under the rug by the major's right foot.

[4]   A heavy, granular powder of red lead oxide that takes fingerprints very well.

[5]   It wasn't just Redl's office that was so decked out; all staff officers of the K.S. had their offices prepared for similar feats of technology.

army, headquartered in Prague, and he brought Redl along with him as his chief of staff. Redl was promptly promoted to colonel—chiefs of intelligence were never given high rank, but now he was back to the real work of a soldier. Pretty good for a boy from a poor and socially invisible family in one of the most caste-ridden armies in Europe. But there were few of his brother officers by then that weren't confidently predicting that someday Alfred Redl would be chief of the Austro-Hungarian General Staff.

Captain Maximilian Ronge took over the job of head of K.S., building on the legacy of efficiency and skill that Redl had left for him. He added several innovations, one of which was a secret postal censorship group called the Black Cabinet. The censors were told that they were on the lookout for customs swindlers; only Ronge, his chief, and the man in charge of the Black Cabinet knew that the real interest was spies.

In 1908 the Austro-Hungarian Empire annexed Bosnia and Herzegovina, a seemingly innocuous flexing of its great-power muscles that gained it the implacable hatred of powerless little Serbia, and put it directly on the road to the confrontation with Russia that became World War I.

On the second of March, 1913, the inspectors in the Black Cabinet came across two letters addressed identically:

Opera Ball, 13,
Poste Restante,
General Post Office,
Vienna

What made them just a bit interesting were their postmarks—both from Eydtkuhnen in East Prussia, near the Russian border.

The Black Cabinet steamed them open, and found Austrian bank notes: One letter held 6,000 kronen, and the other 8,000. Fourteen-thousand kronen, about $US2,700, was a decent year's wages for a working man in 1913. And there was no letter—not so much as a note—in either envelope. Just kronen.

You'd be curious. I'd be curious. The K.S. was *paid* to be curious. They carefully resealed the letters and sent them on.

Captain Ronge had a push button installed at the Poste Restante window of the Vienna post office which rang a bell in the back room of the police station across the street. The clerk on duty was instructed to push the button when someone called for the Opera Ball letters, and stall as long as he could in handing them over. Two detectives were installed across the street to do nothing but wait for the bell to ring.

March passed into April, and April into May. The detectives waited stolidly and patiently, and still nobody called for the letters. On May 24th the bell rang. One of the K.S. men was washing his hands, the other was having a cup of coffee several doors down from the station house. Still they managed to get to the post office in under two minutes.

"You've missed your man!" the clerk told them, pointing at a door to his left. "He left that way a few seconds ago."

The detectives rushed to the street just in time to see a taxi pull away. And it was the only one in sight.

Such a simple job, such an important job, and they had bungled it. The detectives stood there forlornly discussing what to do, unwilling to go in and report failure, for 20 minutes. At which time a taxi pulled up. *The* taxi.

"You drove off with my brother-in-law," one of the detectives told the driver. "Where did you take him?"

"To the Kaiserhof Café."

"Good. Take us there."

On the way to the café the two detectives searched the inside of the taxi. They were products of the Redl system, trained to overlook no possibility, however small. One of them found a grey suede sheath which had slid between the cushions. they examined it and decided that it had held a small pocketknife, of the sort a gentleman might carry. Of course they had no idea how long it had been there, but you never can tell. Thoroughness and attention to details, however small, were part of the Redl system.

When they arrived at the Kaiserhof it was deserted, and the waiters told them that they had had no customers for the past hour and a half. Had their quarry doubled on his tracks? There was another taxi rank near by, and the detectives hurried over. Had anyone taken a cab recently?

An old man who earned his coppers by opening carriage doors remembered that a gentleman had taken a taxi from there about 20 minutes before. And where had he gone?

"Why, the Hotel Klomser, gentlemen. I distinctly heard him say the Hotel Klomser."

The two K.S. agents went to the hotel. "Has anyone checked in in the past half hour?" they asked the portier.

"Yes, several people," the portier told them. "The couple in room 5, Herr Wormser in room 11, a travelling gentleman in room 4, the young lady in room 21, and Colonel Redl in room 1—his usual room when he's here."

"*The* Colonel Redl?" one of the detectives asked.

The portier shrugged. "Colonel Redl of Prague is all I know," he said.

The detective handed the portier the suede sheath. "One of them dropped this," he said. "See if you can find out which one, and give it back. And no need to mention that we're here." He settled down to read a newspaper, while his companion stepped outside.

A few minutes later a dapper gentleman in civilian clothes strolled over to the portier's desk and gave up his key—to room 1.

"Pardon me," said the portier, extending the slip of grey suede, "but has the colonel perhaps mislaid the sheath of his pocket knife?"

"Why, yes," Never were fatal words more casually said. The colonel took the little sheath and started for the door. Halfway there he paused, perhaps remembering where he had lost the sheath. There—in the cab—while slitting open the envelopes with the money. How could the sheath have followed him here?

The detective, peering over his copy of *Simplicissimus*, thought the colonel turned white. But just for a second, and then Redl calmly went out the door.

The detective sprang for the telephone and called 123-408, the number of the Kundschafts Stelle. He relayed the information he had, and then raced outside to help his companion shadow the suspect.

The officers of the K.S. were dumbfounded. *Colonel Redl!* There must be no mistake. Captain Ronge himself rushed to the post office and got the receipt which had been filled out by the man picking up the "Opera Ball, 13," letters. He hurried back to the office and pulled a slim volume from the safe. Written eight years before, in Colonel Redl's own hand, it was a treatise on how to safeguard military secrets while acquiring those of another country.[6]

Captain Ronge compared the handwriting on the receipt with that in the manuscript. They were identical. Was Colonel Redl a traitor? Was there any other possible explanation?

One of the two detectives came into the headquarters bearing a handful of torn scraps of paper. "The colonel tore these up on the Wollnerstrasse and tossed them away," he explained. "I gathered them up."

"Just what the colonel wanted you to do," Captain Ronge said. "He separated you from your companion. It's much easier to escape from only one pursuer."

"We didn't separate," the detective said. "I could see by the way he did it, without looking down, that he didn't care what papers he got, so I assumed he was trying to separate us. We followed him together to the Konkordia Platz, where I took a taxicab, leaving my partner on foot. Only when the suspect had passed up the last of the cab ranks and was clearly headed back to the hotel did I order the cab driver to return to the ripped-up papers."

Captain Ronge had the bits of paper reassembled. They were four post office receipts; one the receipt for the dispatch of money to a Lieutenant Hovora of the Uhlans, and the other three receipts for registered letters to addresses in Brussels, Warsaw, and Lausanne. All three addresses were known to the K.S. as the offices of foreign intelligence services; French, Italian, and Russian.

General August Urbanski von Ostromiecz was the current chief of the Austro-Hungarian Imperial Secret Service, and Captain Ronge's boss. It was Ronge's judgment that, despite the fragmentary, incomplete state of the evidence against Redl, that von Ostromiecz must be notified immediately. It was von Ostromiecz's judgment, later that evening when he had heard the story, that General Conrad von Hötzendorf, commander in chief of the Austro-Hungarian Army, must be told.

General von Hötzendorff was hosting a dinner party at the Grand Hotel. It was the sort of party that pre-war Vienna was famous for; the finest French wines, the world-famous string ensemble of the Grand Hotel, the beautiful women of Vienna, the bravest and handsomest junior officers.

In the midst of dinner a waiter handed him the card of his chief of secret service. "I must speak with you privately," was written on the back. "I am in the office of the hotel manager."

---

6 Organisation der Auskundschaftung fremder Militärverhältnisse und die Abwehr fremder Spionage im Inlande.

The general excused himself and stalked into the manager's office. Interrupted in the middle of dinner—it had better be serious.

It was serious.

General von Hötzendorf and the general staff were the authors of a war plan then sitting in the safe of the general staff. Known as Plan Three, it spelled out exactly what Austria-Hungary would do in a war with Serbia, down to the movement of each individual company—and in some cases each individual soldier. Speed of mobilization and deployment; rail schedules; troop locations; timing of attacks—all were laid out in this master plan of the general staff. Plan Three allowed for the possibility of Russia coming into the war. It had taken years to achieve its final form. It could not easily be changed.

And Colonel Redl, in his post as chief of staff of the Eighth Corps, had access to Plan Three.

"We must hear from his own lips the extent of his treason," von Hötzendorf said.

"It shall be done, Herr General."

"And then," von Hötzendorf turned to von Ostromiecz, "he must die. No one must know the reason for his death. *No one!* Russia must not learn that we know of his treason until we have had time to repair the damage."

"I understand, Herr General."

"See to it, Ostromiecz. You, Captain Ronge, Major Hofer and Wenzel Vorlicek. No one else. Report back to me at once when it is done!"

Colonel Redl dined that evening at the Riedhof with Dr. Victor Pollack, an old friend, and, as it happens, a jurist who often tried espionage cases. The colonel seemed depressed. Men of the K.S. kept him under observation all through the meal, even supplying the waiter who served them in their private room. They overheard nothing of interest.

Redl left the Riedhof and his old friend at 11:30 and returned to the Hotel Klomser. At midnight the four officers, in full uniform, called on him in his room.

Colonel Redl turned away from the table at which he was writing and stood up. "I know why you have come," he said. "I have ruined my life. I am writing letters of farewell."

"We must know the extent of your—activities," von Ostromiecz told him.

"All that you wish to know will be found in my apartment in Prague," Redl said. "May I borrow a revolver?"

Curiously enough none of the officers was armed. One of them went off and returned with a Browning pistol. They handed it to Redl and departed. Leaving one of their number to keep guard on the front door, they retired to the Cafe Central to wait out the night, changing the guard every half-hour. At five in the morning they had one of the detectives who had followed Redl take an envelope up to his room. They told him of what he might find, and warned him to say nothing but merely return to the cafe.

The detective delivered the envelope. Colonel Redl's door was unlocked. The lights were on full. Colonel Redl, the detective judged, had stood in front of the large mirror and watched as he blew his brains out.

The detective snuck out, and the officers called the portier and told him to summon Colonel Redl to the phone, so that the portier would be the one who discovered the body. It was just 13 hours since the two "Opera Ball, 13," letters had been picked up at the Poste Restante window of the general post office.

Colonel Redl left two letters, one addressed to his brother and the other to his mentor, General Baron von Giesl. He also left a note on a half-sheet of paper. Written in a firm, legible hand, it said:

> *Levity and passion have destroyed me. Pray for me. I pay with my life for my sins.*
>
> > *Alfred*
>
> *1:15 A.M. I will die now. Please do not permit an autopsy. Pray for me.*

As soon as von Hötzendorf was informed that Redl was dead, he sent Captain Ronge to Prague to inform General Baron von Giesl of what had happened. The captain and the general went together to Redl's apartment, and found the front door locked with special, strong locks. And they had neglected to bring Redl's keys.

Herr Wagner was the best locksmith in Prague. So, despite the fact that it was Sunday, and he was scheduled to play fullback on his football team, he was drafted for the day.

Herr Wagner opened the front door, and then went around the house, opening drawers, closets, lock boxes, cabinets, and cupboards. They all seemed to be full of paper: reports, maps, documents, photographs, plans, letters, and a lot of cash. But Herr Wagner was not the curious sort; it was no business of his, so he paid no attention.

The officers discovered documents that proved Redl a traitor on a larger scale than any of them could have imagined. In 1902, while he was still chief of the Kundschafts Stelle, he had been blackmailed by the Russians into spying for them. Redl, it seems, was a homosexual.[7] The wealth came after.[8]

---

[7]   To help you understand what a no-no this was then, let me point out that in the books published after the Great War which detailed Redl's perfidy, none of them mentioned this, the weakness of the flesh that had led to his downfall. They talked about his greed, and his need for money, and hinted that there might be more to it, without coming close to stating what the "more" might be. A typical example:

> . . . But Colonel Redl's lust for luxury was anything but respectable in proportion to his income.
> Lust and luxury were with him imperative. He could hide his inner self from his closest colleague. But he made no attempt to hide from himself the fact that his appetites came first and foremost of all the loyalties he recognized.
> —from *Spies*, by Joseph Gollomb, 1928

The key words were all there: "lust," "luxury," "appetites before loyalties," but you had to know already to recognize them. Homosexuality was the taboo of taboos at the time, and even indiscretions that were much less important were blackmailable during a period which regarded honor above all, and had such warped ideas of where honor lay. It is not known how the Russian secret service discovered Colonel Redl's sexual

Once he had resolved, under whatever persuasion, to become a traitor, he went into it whole hog. Plan Three may have been the most important loss, but it didn't stand alone. The apartment was full of secret plans, secret ciphers, confidential army orders, secret reports on the condition of railroads and roads, bridges and tunnels, until it looked like there were no Austrian secrets that Russia was not privy to.

And the best Austro-Hungarian agents in Russia and Serbia—Redl had betrayed them all. Most of them had already been hanged or shot, and now von Giesl knew why.

But the loss of Plan Three proved to be the greatest tragedy. It represented the army's best thinking, and could not easily be changed. When, several months later, a crazed Serbian student fired his pistol at Archduke Franz Ferdinand and his wife, and killed them both, it was too late. War was declared, and Austria-Hungary marched against the Balkan nations.

The empire lost a half-million men in the Balkan campaign, and destroyed itself. The world was dragged into the first, and then a second, global conflict. Of those half-million deaths, the general staff estimated that Redl's treachery was responsible for somewhere between 20 and 30 percent. They did not try to estimate his responsibility for the deaths on the Russian front. Had the Austro-Hungarian General Staff been properly apprised of the strength of Russia's new divisions facing them to the east, there is a chance they might not have gone to war at all. But the agents that could have told them were not in place, thanks to Alfred Redl.

The truth about Colonel Redl was restricted to a list of 10 people—the commander in chief, the chiefs of the War Office and the secret service, and the chief of the Vienna Police—and each of them was required to swear an oath not to repeat what he knew. Even Emperor Franz Joseph himself, even his son and heir Archduke Franz Ferdinand, were not on the list.

The next day the uncurious Wagner was visited by his team captain to discover why he had been missing from the lineup. What could have been more important than playing fullback for Storm I?

Wagner shrugged "I was drafted for the day," he explained. "Had to open a lot of doors and cupboards and stuff in some officer's apartment."

"Some officer?" the team captain—who, in real life was a subeditor on the *Prager Tageblatt*—inquired. "His name wouldn't have been 'Redl,' would it?" He had read the account of the colonel's suicide in Vienna, and wondered about it.

"That's it," Wagner agreed. "He had a lot of Russian papers about; and maps, and photographs, and an awful lot of money."

Press censorship in Prague was very strict. To print what he now believed would have landed the subeditor-football captain in jail, along with most of

---

preferences, but that surely must rank as one of the most important intelligence coups of all time.

[8]   Redl holds the record for having received the largest payment to a spy that is known—in today's money, over a quarter of a million dollars. But Plan Three was certainly worth the expense.

the staff of the paper. But Czechs had become very adept at reading between the lines. He and his editor stayed up that night constructing the proper lines. And, on Tuesday, May 27, 1913, they blew the Redl story wide open:

> We are asked by a high authority to contradict rumors which have been spread, particularly in army circles, about the Chief of the Staff of the Prague Army Corps, Colonel A. Redl, who, as already reported, committed suicide in Vienna on Sunday morning. The rumors are to the effect that the colonel had been guilty of betraying military secrets to a foreign Power, believed to be Russia. As a matter of fact, the commission of high officers who came to Prague to carry out a search in the dead colonel's house were investigating quite another matter.

Quite.

13 MATA HARI

Born in Java of a rich Dutch father married to a famous Javanese beauty, who died giving birth to her, the girl was taken to India at the age of 14 and placed in the temple of the mystic cult called Kanda Swandi. The priests named her Mata Hari, "Eye of the Morning," for her beauty, and dedicated her to Siva. They began training her to dance, and to perform the other rites demanded of a temple virgin.

When she was 16 she was stolen from the temple by Sir Campbell McLeod, an officer in the British Army, who had seen her dance and fallen in love with her.

Sir Campbell and Mata Hari McLeod lived well in India, where she gave birth to a son and daughter. The native gardener poisoned the boy, so Mata Hari killed him with her husband's revolver. She and her husband and her little daughter had to flee to Europe. Once there, her husband died of a sudden relapse of fever. The daughter went to a convent and Mata Hari had to do something to support herself, but she didn't know what. What was she trained for?

"I finally decided," she related in her journal, "by means of the dance to interpret the soul of the Orient to the rest of the world." And so she did. Her interpretive dancing soon became the rage of Europe, and she became the darling of the nobility.

One day in Berlin she was asked by a personage high in the kaiser's government to entertain a Russian ambassador. She moved into a richly furnished mansion in Dorotheen strasse, and assumed the name "Countess von Linden." Without realizing it, and against her will, she was now in the toils of the Imperial German Secret Service; toils from which no man—or woman—can escape except by death. "That," she wrote, "was how I became a spy."

That's the way Mata Hari told it. But let's start again.

Margaret Gertrude Zelle was born in Leeuwarden, Holland, the daughter of Adam and Antje Zelle, on August 7, 1876. She attended a convent school, and when she was 18 married a Dutch captain (of Scottish ancestry) named McLeod. They went to Java, where he was put in charge of a colonial army reserve. He was in his forties, an alcoholic, and a mean drunk. When drunk he would beat her and wave his loaded revolver in her face. When he was sober he would send her to his fellow officers to borrow money. He never asked her what the terms of such loans were.

In 1901 they returned to Europe with a little daughter, Marie Louise. The child was placed in a Dutch convent, and Margaret divorced her husband. She supported herself by dancing. She must have studied Javanese temple dancing while in the East Indies, for she was good at it. The legend is that she was unbelievably beautiful; but there are photographs. Even allowing for the plumper standards of the time, Mata was at best passable looking.

But she danced nude.

She would do her version of the dance of the seven veils, spinning herself out of layer after layer of diaphanous gauze until only her breastplates remained. It was called art, and she was a minor sensation.

In the first decade of the 20th Century public nudity was rare enough to be a powerful aphrodisiac, and Mata Hari had many rich and powerful lovers—none of them for very long, it seems, but as she moved about Europe from one capital city to the next, they sufficed.

She had noble—even royal—lovers in Berlin, the crown prince among them. Also Von Jagow, the chief of police. It is possible that, in 1910, she went to the German espionage school at Lorrach. Not probable, but possible. The story of the mansion in Dorotheen strasse may well be true in outline, if not in substance. There was such a house, kept by the German Secret Service, and the various women who called it home entertained such foreigners as could be lured there to spend the night.

But she seems to have been too flighty for steady intelligence work, so she went on with her dancing, and her admirers, and an occasional job for the German Secret Service. Or possibly she merely accepted presents from her German lovers, and they found it convenient to bill the account of the secret service. At any rate she was, apparently, listed as agent H.21 in the records of the German Secret Service.

There are many stories about Mata Hari's spying for the German Secret Service, using her body to lure French and British officers to betray their

Courtesy of CULVER PICTURES

Mata Hari

countries. Most of these stories are romantic nonsense, and the remainder are utter nonsense.[1]

At some time during Mata Hari's stay in Paris during the war, the Deuxième Bureau, the French counterintelligence service, decided that she was a dangerous spy. They had a dossier on her from before the war. She had been noted in a carriage in Berlin with Chief of Police Von Jagow, who was now chief of the German intelligence service. She had slept with[2] many important officials, both German and French. She danced in the nude.

In 1915 the Italian Secret Service had sent a memo to the secret services of all the allied powers:

> While examining the passenger list of a Japanese vessel at Naples we have recognized the name of a theatrical celebrity from Marseilles named Mata Hari, the famous Hindu dancer, who purports to reveal secret Hindu dances which demand total nudity. She has, it seems, renounced her claim to Indian birth and become Berlinoise. She speaks German with a slight Eastern accent.

Well. Now the French were convinced that she was a spy. After all, some Italian Secret Service agent on the docks of Naples said she had become Berlinoise.

The French *knew* that she had lived in Berlin. They even knew that she knew Von Jagow, which is more than the Italians knew. They must have known that she spoke German. (And what is that business about the "slight Eastern accent?" She was Dutch.) But it took a telegram from Italy to convince them that the lady was a spy.

They took to watching her. They admitted that she did not behave like a spy—no mysterious meetings, no furtive behavior, completely open with everything, even her amours. But was that not, in itself, suspicious?

She applied for a pass to visit the town of Vittel, where a former lover, Captain Maroff, was lying blinded in a hospital. But was Vittel not near where a military flying field was being established?[3] While there she made friends with the pilots. Was that not suspicious?

---

[1]   For instance: Mata Hari, wearing a dress showing extreme décollété and waving a large fan, was dining with an officer of the merchant marine on a certain Tuesday. She told him that she desired a small gift from him—a Spanish mantilla. He promised.

"When will I get it?" she demanded.

"I'll wire my agents in Barcelona," he assured her. "The Corona will sail Thursday at midnight. You should have it by Saturday."

She spread her fan three-quarters open and fanned herself with it. "You are good to me," she murmured.

At the next table a man was watching. He noted how far Mata Hari's fan was spread, which direction it was pointing, and how many times she fanned it. Later that evening he called someone in Brest and talked about his uncle's bout with pneumonia.

From Brest went a telegram to Holland about canned food. From Holland went a coded message over the short wave.

And on Thursday a waiting U-boat torpedoed and sank the Corona. Fifteen Allied ships were sunk by such means.

That's the story. It is implausible in every detail, impossible in several. Try, for example, to devise a fan code that could pass on the name of a ship, the date and time of its

Mata Hari was called in to be interrogated by the Deuxième Bureau; there she was threatened with deportation. She protested her innocence. She told them she had German lovers, but that her soul was French. She offered to spy for France, if they would have her. They pretended to believe her protestations (But the woman dances *nude!* How can one trust her?). Since one of her German lovers, General von Bissing, was in Belgium, they sent her there, providing her with a list of six agents to contact. They were agents that the French didn't trust anyway, so what happened to them would be a good sign of Mata Hari's sincerity.

Shortly one of the six agents was arrested by the Germans and shot as a spy. Was there a connection, or was it a coincidence? A lot of people in Belgium were being rounded up by the Germans and shot as spies. If Mata Hari had indeed turned the list over to the Germans, what about the other five, who had not been arrested? Well, maybe they were double agents.

At any rate, after a stopover in London, where she was interviewed by Sir Basil Thompson, head of Scotland Yard, Mata Hari went on to Madrid[4].

Her lovers in Madrid were Captains von Kalle and Canaris, the German naval attachés,[5] and Von Kron, the military attaché. But secret service funds were low, and Mata Hari was an expensive luxury. Captain von Kalle suggested that Mata Hari go back to Paris, but she didn't want to go. He arranged for a payment of 15,000 pesetas to be awaiting her in Paris, perhaps as an inducement for her to go. And so she went. Unfortunately the secret service instructions for agent H.21 to go to Paris were sent in a code that the French had penetrated.[6]

Mata Hari went to the Hotel Plaza Athenée in Paris, where she was promptly arrested.

After a preliminary hearing, she was taken to the prison of Saint-Lazare and placed in cell number 12, which had previously housed Mme. Caillaux, who had shot the editor of *le Figaro*, Mme. Steinheil, who had murdered a president of the republic, and Marguerette Francillard, who had been executed as a spy.

---

sailing, and the port it sails from, and still appear natural to anyone watching. And, after you've done that, explain why she didn't just drop him a note. And—but no, I'll leave the rest of the dissection to you, if you care. Truth is not stranger than fiction; much of the time truth is fiction.

[2] "Bestowed her favors on," was the way they put it.

[3] It would have been difficult in 1916 to go anywhere in France that was not near some other place of military importance.

[4] Sir Basil, after listening to her story, advised her to give up espionage. She thanked him for the advice.

[5] Captain Walter Wilhelm Canaris later became head of the Abwehr, the German military intelligence bureau, and was executed in 1944 for his part in a plot against Hitler.

[6] And that the Germans knew the French had penetrated.

On July 24, 1917, Mata Hari was tried by secret court-martial for being a German spy. There is no doubt that the sentence was sure before the trial began.

The three judges, Colonel Semprou, commander of the Garde Républicain, Major Massard, and Lieutenant Mornet, were convinced of her guilt. The presentation of evidence was a mere formality to taking her out and shooting her.

Maitre Clunet, who was appointed her counsel by the Corporation of Barristers, became convinced of her innocence. He did a magnificent job of defending her, but he was banging his head against the stone wall of Gallic intransigence. The judges knew her to be guilty, and they were not about to be swayed by contrary evidence.

She had received 30,000 marks from Von Jagow, the chief of police of Berlin shortly after the war started. Yes, she was still in Berlin, yes, she was still seeing him—but *30,000 marks!*

"He was my lover," she said simply. "That was the price of my favors."

"This amount seems rather large for a simple gift," Colonel Semprou commented.

"Not to me," she replied.[7]

She admitted continuing to write to her German lover, who was now head of the secret service in Holland, but insisted that, "It is not my fault that he had that appointment. But I wrote nothing about the war. He got no information from me."[8]

She defended her befriending soldiers, saying that she did it sometimes out of sympathy, sometimes for money. "Harlot, yes —but traitress, never!" she insisted. "After all," she told the court, "I am not French. I have the right to cultivate any relations that may please me. The war is not a sufficient reason to stop me from being a cosmopolitan."

The court-martial did not agree. On October 15, at five o'clock in the morning, Margaret Zelle McLeod was taken to the rifle-range at Vincennes where the sentence of execution was read aloud, as prescribed by law. Witnesses relate that she was resigned and unafraid.[9] She was loosely tied to a tree. She declined a blindfold. At 5:47, she was shot by a 12-man firing squad.

France at the time was suffering from mutiny in the ranks and defeatism at home. Examples had to be made. Mata Hari was an example. Maitre Clunet's attempts to get her clemency were ignored. The prime minister of

---

[7]   Had she known it she could have told the court that in 1914 the German secret service did not have an extra 30,000 marks to spend on the Dutch courtesan. The money was clearly out of Von Jagow's own pocket—and at the time the police chief had nothing to do with the secret service.

[8]   The Deuxième Bureau, which had copies of many of these letters, did not produce them. Presumably there was nothing incriminating in them.

[9]   It has been suggested that she had been told—and believed—that the bullets were to be blanks, and that she would be allowed to escape. But there is no reason for either her or us to believe that.

Courtesy of CULVER PICTURES

Darstellung der Erschießung Mata Haris
in einem englischen Magazin.

A drawing of Mata Hari's execution.

Holland, van der Linden, suggested to the queen that she sign an appeal for this lady, one of her subjects, who didn't seem to have done anything really wrong. But the queen had heard about Mata Hari's many lovers, about her dancing in the nude, and firmly refused.

Even before her death the legends had begun to grow. They have never stopped.

14 MAJOR WILLIAM MARTIN

One of the most successful intelligence "agents" of World War II was Captain (acting major) William Martin of the Royal Marines. And the most remarkable fact about this most unusual man is that he never existed.

In April of 1943 the British and Americans were well on their way to gaining control of North Africa, and were preparing to invade what Winston Churchill called the "soft under-belly of Europe." The only problem was, where? There were only a few good points on which to land an invasion force, and the Germans and Italians knew where they were as well as the British and Americans. The south of France, Italy, and Greece were the best bets. The Axis could defend all of them well enough to make any invasion attempt a chancy proposition; but if they knew for certain at which point the invasion was aimed, they could mass enough armor, artillery, and air power to drive it back into the sea.

The obverse of that was that if the Allies could convince the Axis[1] that they were landing somewhere else, and draw off even one tank division, it would ensure the success of the landing and save thousands of lives.

---

[1]   Originally the "Rome-Berlin Axis," by 1936 it was abbreviated "Axis." This term came to include Germany, Italy, Japan, and their allies in World War Two.

The Allies decided to launch their invasion at Sicily, the large island that sticks out from the boot of Italy. There were many reasons why this was the logical choice: It was comparatively close to points on the coast of North Africa from which ships could sail, so the invasion fleet wouldn't have too much open sea to cover. Fighter planes, which have limited range, could use air bases in North Africa to protect the island beachheads from air attack. Sicily would be defended mainly by Italian troops, who gave every sign of not really wanting to be in this war anyway.

The only problem, of course, was that every one of those reasons was known to the Axis,[2] which made them tend to defend Sicily more heavily. Which put more German tank divisions, artillery battalions, and dive-bomber squadrons around the beachheads in Sicily than the Allies really wanted to meet on the first day or so of an invasion. Coming ashore in one of those flat-bottom barges was difficult enough without facing any extra armor or artillery as you waded through the surf.

As Ewen Montagu[3] put it:

> As soon as the operations in North Africa began, we had to decide what the next operation would be. For us there was no doubt that this was Sicily, and we began to realize that this would seem equally obvious to the German General Staff. Since the Mediterranean is not too large a sea, shaped like a figure of eight because of several straits in the centre, we knew it would be impossible to land in Italy, France or Greece without first neutralizing Sicily and closing down its airports. So we had to think carefully and find a way to convince the highly professional German General Staff that we intended to undertake something which was in fact impossible.

Montagu came up with a scheme which, if it worked, might have the desired effect.[4] It was code-named "Mincemeat."

The basic idea was an age-old stratagem of war: planting false information with the enemy. Attila the Hun,[5] in the fifth century, held a parade of his cavalry before the emissaries of some of his enemies. What they couldn't know was that the paraders, once past the reviewing area, would gallop around in a great circle and come up at the end of the line again. The emissaries reported that the forces of Attila seemed endless. Moving forward 1,200 years: When the American Revolutionary Army was

---

2   "Anybody but a damn fool," Churchill said, "will know it's Sicily!"

3   Lt. Cmdr. Ewen Montagu was at the time in Section 17F of the British Admiralty, the department of Naval Intelligence in charge of deception operations. It was he who invented "Major Martin," and who, in 1954, wrote *The Man Who Never Was*, the first book detailing the operation.

4   The use of the two qualifiers "if" and "might" in the same sentence will serve to show how chancy everyone thought the scheme. But if it did work, ah then, what tunes of glee might be sung in the corridors of the Admiralty.!

5   "Attila, the Scourge of God, King of the Huns," as his hordes called him.

encamped in Morristown in 1777, it was reported to General Washington that the British had a spy in the camp. Instead of having him arrested, Washington ordered his staff officers to befriend the man and pretend to believe his cover story. The spy wandered about the camp until he came upon a staff officer's tent. On the portable desk in the tent just happened to be the strength reports of every brigade in the Continental Army. The spy stole the reports and brought them to the British General Howe. The reports, as I'm sure you've guessed, were phony. For a year Howe thought the American forces to be twice as large as they really were, and treated them with undue respect.

And then of course there was the Meinertzhagen Haversack Gambit,[6] which had proven so useful in World War I. But would anyone fall for it again? The trick was so old that it couldn't fool anyone. Unless it were given a new twist. . . .

"Supposing," Montagu suggested to those few people with whom he was allowed to discuss such things, "that the Germans find papers on a corpse suggesting that the landings will take place somewhere else. Someone who apparently died in a plane crash. They'd believe that, wouldn't they?"[7]

A plane crash, it turned out, wouldn't do. Since presumably they would have to start out with a corpse—and where to obtain a corpse?—instead of crashing a plane with a living person on it, an autopsy would show that the wounds caused by the plane crash were inflicted after death. That would blow the whole charade.

Suppose it were made to look as though the plane went down at sea, and the victim lived through it but died subsequently of, say, exposure?

Montagu went to talk with Sir Bernard Spilsbury, the Home Office pathologist, and probably the most knowledgeable man in Great Britain on what a body would look like after going through the indignity of any particular form of death. It was, Spilsbury allowed, possible, under the right conditions. If someone wearing a life jacket went into the sea and was not rescued in a short time he would probably faint from the cold.[8] In a short time he would either freeze to death or drown. In either case there would be no external marks.

Montagu and his compatriots now went about finding the body, and determining just what to do with it. It was decided that the corpse should be that of a military officer, probably a Royal Marine,[9] that he should be carrying a briefcase full of important papers, and that he should appear in the sea

---

6   See chapter 16.

7   These quotes are all made up. The people quoted must have said something like this at the time, but their exact words are lost to posterity. The facts are true.

8   A given temperature of water is much more severe on the body than the same temperature of air; water conducts heat better than air, and the body is unable to retain its internal temperature.

9   The army was rejected because it was so large that signals and inquiries about the supposed officer could not be restricted. The navy was rejected because a naval officer would not be wearing battledress, and it would cause too many questions to have a corpse fitted for a dress uniform. The Royal Marines won the honor by default.

off the coast of Spain. The Spanish were neutral, but leaning heavily toward Germany, and several towns in Spain had active Abwehr agents with good connections in the local government.

A body was found, that of a man in his twenties who had died of pneumonia in a London hospital. As the man was unmarried, Montagu asked his parents for permission to use the body "for a worthwhile purpose." He must have been convincing, for the parents agreed, with the two provisos that the body would receive a Christian burial, and that its true identity would never be revealed.[10]

Montagu went back to Sir Bernard Spilsbury, who approved the body. Pneumonia was a stroke of luck, as there would be some liquid in the lungs. A post mortem examination by a doctor, who already had the preconceived notion that the corpse had died of drowning, would not note the difference between that fluid and seawater.

At any rate: "You have nothing to fear from a Spanish *post mortem*," Sir Bernard told Montagu. "To detect that this young man had not died after an aircraft had been lost at sea would need a pathologist of my experience—and there aren't any in Spain."

It was now that "Mincemeat" was officially on, and "Major William Martin" came into existence. There were enough Martins on the Royal Marines active duty list so that one more would not attract undue attention. And William was a common first name. Major William Martin's name would have to be put on the casualty list if the Germans were to be expected to believe in his body, and an uncommon name might be difficult to explain away.[11]

Montagu put together the letters and documents with which to stuff the briefcase and pockets, and create the illusion of William Martin. The Germans would have to believe in Major Martin if they were to believe that he had crashed at sea bearing important secret papers.

An identity card with Major Martin's picture was needed. They tried photographing the corpse, but, as Montagu put it, "It is impossible to describe how utterly and hopelessly dead any photograph of the body looked." By pure luck Montagu spotted a man who looked like a double for the major, and talked him into sitting for an identity card photograph. Then a pass was issued for Major Martin to enter Combined Operations[12] Headquarters, where he supposedly worked.

But more was needed to establish Major Martin as a real person. Montagu

---

[10]   And, to this day, it has not been.

[11]   It wasn't just a problem of possible German thoroughness. The Royal Marines was not so large that the appearance of an unusual, but never-before-seen name on the casualty list wouldn't be remarked.

[12]   Combined Operations Command used men from all services working together to stage raids on the coast of occupied Europe. These men became known as the "Commandos."

[13]   In translation. And, indeed, translations of the letters were found, along with a long

decided that the major should be engaged to a girl named Pam. He had two love letters written by a girlfriend of a secretary in his office, letters that were so real and so poignant that no one who read them would doubt that there was a Major Martin, or that "Pam" was in love with him. A photograph of "Pam," along with the bill for the engagement ring, a letter from Major Martin's "father," two ticket stubs from the Prince of Wales Theatre, a bill for his last night's stay from the Naval and Military Club, and an overdraft letter from his bank were all prepared to be put in Major Martin's pockets.

And now the meat of the matter. What documents would convince the German military that the main thrust of the coming invasion was not Sicily but—say—Sardinia? And then a second and heavier invasion against Greece?

The first instinct would be to send phoney battle plans and orders. The first instinct of German intelligence would be to doubt battle plans and orders. If you want someone to believe something, let him ferret it out for himself. He will feel so clever at having discovered it, that it will be hard for him to disown it even in the face of contrary evidence.

What about personal letters from one high-ranking officer to another—letters that just hint at the coming campaign? They would have the added advantage, Captain Montagu felt, of being included in the report that the Abwehr agent sent to his bosses in Berlin.[13] What agent could resist sending along a personal letter from General Nye to General Alexander—or from Lord Mountbatten to Admiral of the Fleet Sir A.B. Cunningham?

Montagu asked Lord Mountbatten and General Nye to supply appropriate letters, and they did excellent jobs. The letters, along with a set of proofs for a book called COMBINED OPERATIONS, the Official Story of the Commandos,[14] were put in a briefcase, which was chained to Major Martin by a chain of the sort bank messengers use: It was attached to his belt, and then went up and out one sleeve.

There was a bit of discussion about the chain. It was needed to make sure the briefcase didn't just float off or sink. But Royal Marine officers didn't put their briefcases on chains. Then it occurred to someone that the Germans didn't know that. And besides, if Major Martin had wanted to, for reasons of security, nobody would have stopped him.

Major Martin's uniform was prepared,[15] and put on the body, one of the more unpleasant jobs of the whole operation. The pockets were filled with

---

Intelligence "appreciation," in the Abwehr files in Berlin after the war.

14   A real book, included for an air of verisimilitude. Martin was suposedly carrying the proofs for General Eisenhower to examine, and then say a few kind words about, before the United States edition was published. A letter to that effect was included with the proofs.

15   Not only was care taken over details like the underwear being properly watermarked, but, as Martin was only an acting major, his trench coat shoulder straps were first pierced for the three pips of a captain before the major's crown was affixed.

what Major Martin might be expected to be carrying,[16] and everything was checked one last time before Major Martin was wrapped in a blanket and lowered into a prepared canister. Then dry ice was packed all around the body, and the top was sealed.[17]

The canister, which was labeled "Optical Instruments," was taken to the submarine *Seraph*, and loaded aboard.

At 4:30 in the morning of the 3rd of May, 1943, the *Seraph* surfaced in the Atlantic about a mile off the southern coast of Spain, near the fishing village of Huelva. The canister was opened and the body was removed. One of the ship's officers blew up the "Mae West" lifejacket, and Major William Martin of the Royal Marines went to war.

Huelva had been selected for the drop because a particularly energetic Abwehr agent was known to be at work there. Although only a small fishing village, it was close enough to the British naval base at Gibraltar to be a useful observation post.

Late that afternoon the body was picked up by a fishing boat and brought ashore. It was turned over to a young intern for the postmortem, and he did a careful job. The major had drowned, he concluded, and the body had been drifting in the sea for five or six days. It was given a full military burial, with Spanish military and civil authorities present, in addition to the British vice-consul.

But the papers?

There had been no briefcase with the body when it was returned to the vice-consul. London immediately sent a message to the ambassador in Madrid, Sir Samuel Hoare, to make discreet requests of the Spanish Admiralty to establish what had happened to the papers.

In the meantime the Abwehr office in Madrid had the papers. They photocopied them and resealed them in the envelopes. Copies were immediately sent to Berlin.

The next day the briefcase was turned over to the British ambassador. The letters were all inside, and their seals seemed to be intact. The briefcase and its contents were sent back to London for scientific analysis.

At least two of the letters, it was concluded, had been opened and then carefully resealed. There was even evidence of clamp marks where the letters had been held down to be photographed.

The chiefs of staff in London sent a message to Churchill, who was in Washington: "Mincemeat swallowed whole!"

On May 15, 1943, the German First Panzer (Tank) Division was moved from the south of France to Greece. On May 20 the German navy began lay-

---

[16]   In addition to the mentioned letters and bills, the following items were included: identity discs, silver cross on silver chain around neck, wristwatch; wallet containing the identity card, the pass, the photograph and the letters from his fiancee, along with a book of stamps (two used); one five-pound note and three one-pound notes, one half-crown, two shillings, two sixpences, four pennies, two bus tickets, two theater ticket stubs, a box of matches, a pack of cigarettes, a bunch of keys, and a pencil stub.

[17]   The carbon dioxide from the evaporating dry ice would slow down the decomposition of the body.

ing additional minefields around the Greek islands, and the army began increasing the fortifications along the coast. Field Marshal Keitel moved additional tank units to Sardinia and Corsica. In early June a flotilla of R-boats were sent from Sicily to Greece.

Even two weeks after the invasion of Sicily had begun, Hitler was still convinced that it was a diversion, and he sent Field Marshal Rommel to Salonica to supervise the defenses against the coming attack.

How many lives Major Martin saved is impossible to estimate—certainly hundreds, probably thousands. And he shortened the war by many months.

He lies to this day in a little graveyard in Huelva. His headstone reads:

> *WILLIAM MARTIN*
> *BORN 29TH MARCH 1907*
> *DIED 24TH APRIL 1943*
> *BELOVED SON OF JOHN*
> *GLYNDWYR MARTIN AND*
> *THE LATE ANTONIA MARTIN*
> *OF CARDIFF, WALES*
> Dulce et decorum est
> pro patria mori.
> RIP

15 ELSBETH SCHRAGMÜLLER

It is subtly and almost accidentally that legends are born.[1] When the First World War broke out in August, 1914, Fräulein Doktor Elsbeth Schragmüller[2] wanted to serve her country.[3] She was only 26 years old, but that was far older than the young male recruits going to the front, and there must be something useful that she, with her fine, trained intellect, could do. Nursing didn't interest her. She wanted to fight—or come as close as the authorities would allow.

The authorities allowed her to proceed to Brussels, recently captured in the first major offensive of the war, and work in the censorship bureau. She proved to have the sort of eye for detail that might be expected of a recent "Doktor" of "Philosophie," and an innate sense of what sort of information might be useful to the intelligence department of an army at war.

---

[1]   I have pieced this story together from what seem to me to be the best sources. There are, as you will see further on, other possibilities for how this story should go.

[2]   Her doctorate was in philosophy, from the University of Freiburg. The title of her dissertation, for you completists, was *Die Bruderschaft der Borer und Balierer von Freiburg und Waldkirch*. It was a study of ancient Teutonic guilds.

[3]   Germany.

Courtesy of CULVER PICTURES

German staff officers reviewing the troops in Antwerp, March 1915. Second from right has been identified as General von Beseler. There are no known photographs of Fräulein Doktor Schragmüller (but see chapter 9 for a fictive image).

The siege of Antwerp was under way when General von Beseler, commander of the army corps investing that city, noted the good material being supplied from the censorship bureau—much of it signed "Schragmüller."

"Who is this Lieutenant Schragmüller?" he asked Captain Refer, one of his intelligence officers. "The fellow has a good head for the sort of information the Army needs. Have him report to me!"

The next day a slender blonde girl with intense blue eyes showed up in Von Beseler's headquarters, insisting that the general had sent for her. After the initial surprise was sorted out, Von Beseler sat her down and congratulated her. "Your reports show a considerable grasp of military strategy and tactics," he said. "I am recommending you for promotion to the Nachrichtendienst."[4]

---

4   Secret Service.

5   At Lorrach, under Spymaster Fredrich Gruber; at Wesel; and at Baden-Baden, which had the best climate and, under Major Joseph Salonek, was responsible for coordinating the German and Austro-Hungarian secret services. It is not known which one or ones "Fräulein Doktor" attended.

On October 9, 1914, Antwerp surrendered to the German Army and "Fräulein Doktor" Schragmüller left her duties at the censorship bureau and went to one of the three special schools run by the German Secret Service for training their agents.[5] And then, although there are no records to verify this, she probably went to another of the schools. And then, quite possibly, to the third. It is known that she was an exemplary student, finding the memorizing of British and French unit designations, and learning how to use secret codes and secret inks and all the other minutiae of the spy, to be much less demanding then the mastery of German philosophy.

By the time she graduated she had so impressed her instructors that, although she had no field experience, she was sent to Antwerp to teach at the new spy school that was being established there, under the direction of an Intelligence veteran named Major Groos. This school was of vital importance, training the agents that would be sent against Great Britain, the French channel ports, and Holland.[6]

The location of Major Groos's spy school was an old mansion at 10 rue de la Pepinière,[7] an address that the Antwerpians soon learned to avoid. Not that the Belgians had any idea of what was going on inside its stone walls, but they quickly noticed that if one so much as stopped to admire the shape of the portico, a German Military Police patrol would suddenly appear and insist upon knowing one's interest in the building, one's current business in the area, and one's family history back for several generations. And if you thought that average German soldiers had no sense of humor—well!—they were practically the Marx Brothers compared to the Military Police.

Agents sent for training to the Antwerp school arrived in closed cars, with shades over the side-windows. When they entered the school they gave up their names, which were replaced with code names, written on white cards and affixed to the doors of their bedrooms, where they were kept locked up for the first three weeks. They lived and worked alone, to assure that they could not recognize, and thus betray, those studying alongside them. After three weeks those who had not yet washed out of the school could leave their bedrooms, but they were still supposed to avoid each other.

At first they studied the tools of modern warfare, from handguns to field artillery, from merchant ships to battleships and submarines, and all the myriad of technical information necessary in all these fields. And then "Fräulein Doktor" herself took over, to teach them codes and ciphers and secret inks, and the little tricks and dodges that can mean the difference between life and death to the working spy in wartime. Her hints were valuable, and many still hold today. For example:[8]

---

6   Which was neutral, but never mind.

7   With a side entrance at 33 rue de l'Harmonie for the shy.

8   As quoted by an Antwerp graduate who ignored her precepts sufficiently to be caught and tried.

Conceal whatever linguistic gifts you have to encourage others to talk more freely in your hearing. And remember; no German agent speaks or writes a word of German while on duty abroad, and this applies even if German is manifestly not your native tongue.

or:

When obtaining information by direct bargaining, make your informant travel as far as possible away from his home—and away from your immediate field of operations as well. Try to have him travel the distance by a tedious route, preferably at night. A tired informant is less cautious or suspicious, more relaxed and expansive, less disposed to lie, or to bargain shrewdly—all advantages in the transaction which you reserve to yourself.

It was now that the legends concerning "Fräulein Doktor" began—and quickly grew. Major Groos may have been the headmaster, but the blonde "Doktor" got all the publicity. She was cruel, her adversaries said, cruel, cunning, and ruthless. She, it was claimed, originated the heartless practice of the "fool spy," the inept or untrustworthy agent who is sent on a mission to be captured or killed, and so distract the counterintelligence officers from other agents.[9] An incompetent Dutch agent named Hoegnagel was caught in Paris trying to pass a newspaper with a coded message written in the margin. French counterintelligence promptly tried him, shot him, and blamed "Fräulein Doktor." She was heartless and cold-blooded, and had deliberately "sacrificed" this poor dupe of a Dutchman. But, if they *really* felt that way, why did they shoot him? She was omniscient, the Entente[10] counterintelligence forces reported, and very dangerous. She may or may not have ever gone into the field, but her enemies reported finding her everywhere. Once "Mademoiselle le Docteur" was detected in six places at once, all over the continent. When the United States entered the war, it was not long before she was being regularly discovered in America.

To add to the confusion, the true identity of "Fräulein Doktor" was not known, and Major Groos was graduating a fair number of attractive blonde agents from the Antwerp academy. Every officer of every Entente counterespionage service wanted the glory of capturing "Fräulein Doktor," and many of them claimed it. She was variously identified as one Gertrud Wurtz; as "a pretty little thing" named Felice Schmidt; and as Irma Staub, "noblewoman and patriot adventuress."[11] At the end of the war a lady ex-spy named Anna-Marie Lesser broke down and admitted, less than truthfully, that *she* had been the notorious "Fräulein Doktor."

---

9   Doktor Schragmüller may or may not have had anything to do with the use of this practice in the Antwerp School, but she certainly didn't originate it; it antedates her by at least a thousand years.

10   The word means "agreement" or "understanding" in French. The "Entente Cordiale," established in 1904 between England and France was broadened to a "Triple Entente," including Russia, in 1907. The word "Entente" was therefore used to describe these allied powers as well as their alliance during the First World War.

After the war "Fräulein Doktor" disappeared, and Elsbeth Schragmüller went on with her life, her secret identity safe in the most secret archives of the German Secret Service. The closest she came to a commendation was a remark by Colonel Nicolai, famed head of the Nachrichtendienst for many years: "It is remarkable that in the German Intelligence Service it was a cavalry officer of an old family and an unusually well-educated woman who knew best how to deal with the agents, even the most difficult and crafty of them." It is not known who the cavalry officer was, but the well-educated woman was most assuredly "Fräulein Doktor" Elsbeth Schragmüller.

The romance continued in the years after the war, as various spies and counterspies wrote their memoirs. Many of them had strangely inaccurate views of espionage for people who claimed to have done it, but it is a field where one's credentials are hard to check. Every one of them had known the notorious and mysterious "Fräulein Doktor," and was prepared to reveal it. And, curiously, each of them revealed a different lady. Captain Henry Landau,[12] of the British Secret Service, whose wartime experiences make good reading, came close, but missed in several essential details. In a book called *All's Fair*, published in 1934, he reveals that:

> The German Secret Service in Belgium was under the direction of a mysterious woman, known as Frau [sic] Doktor, and under a dozen other names. She was at different times said to be the daughter of a noble family, an old cocotte, and the mistress of a German General, whose influence had secured for her the appointment. The truth about her is that she won her appointment by merit; she did come of a good family but quarreled with them over a love affair. Thrown on her own, she eventually drifted into the peace-time German Secret Service, did brilliant work as an agent in France, and showed such remarkable ability and intelligence that eventually she was awarded the post in Belgium. She was a good-looking, buxom, middle-aged woman, with the disposition of a tiger. From her headquarters in Antwerp, she sent many an agent into England and France. It was said of her that she shot with her own hand one or two agents who had played her false, and that she deliberately sent into a trap others she wished to get rid of . . . Her policy was to make her agents so thoroughly afraid of her that fear of vengeance would deter them from treachery.

Edwin T. Woodhall,[13] in a book called *Spies of the Great War* that reads a lot like an E. Phillips Oppenheim spy novel, got it all wrong:

---

11   Who supposedly chose her "common" cover name to spare the feelings of her noble relatives.

12   O.B.E., Croix de Guerre, Chevalier Order of the Crown of Belgium.

13   Late Special Branch of the C.I.D. and Scotland Yard. Author of *Detective and Secret Service Days*.

"The Lady Doctor," the brilliant German woman spy, was originally
destined for the profession of surgery and medicine, and graduated
several colleges for this purpose . . .

She first came under notice of the Russian Secret Service in Vienna
in 1908, during the time of the annexation of Bosnia and Herzegovina.
She attracted the interest of the French during the Agadir crisis of 1911
in Morocco. In 1912, she was the object of English observation, and her
movements were well noted in this country by our Secret Service. She
specialized more in diplomatic matters than in military or naval. But
she was versatile in any category of espionage work.

I recall seeing her upon two occasions, once in 1912, and once again,
the last time, in the Spring of 1914. She was an exceptionally beautiful
creature . . . But in this country she met with no success as a spy, so far
as I can ascertain. She was too well marked. Any success she may have
attained was in France or Russia—particularly the latter . . .

It was a pigeon message she sent from her hotel behind the Russian
front that led Hindenburg's General Staff to deduce the position of the
advancing Russians. A surprise attack upon the centre and flank by
the Germans drove a wedge between the two Russian Armies, which
ended in a precipitate retreat, and final disaster in the Mazurian
Swamps; and the Russian disaster at Tannenberg made a complete
triumph for Germany.

Unhappily for *"Le Docteur,"* as the Russians were retreating she was
seen by an officer of the Russian Secret Service, who recognized her as
a German woman spy of Vienna in 1908. She was arrested, denounced
and shot as a spy. Her beautiful body was probably still warm as the
victorious German cavalry galloped into the town, just twenty minutes
too late to save the life of one of the cleverest women spies who had
served in the ranks of their Secret Service.

Herbert Yardley, known as a codebreaker and poker player, describes in
his *The American Black Chamber,* "the famous German spy, Madame
Maria de Victorica, alias Marie de Vussière, the beautiful blonde woman of
Antwerp." Can we detect here, as in a funhouse mirror, the face of Elsbeth
Schragmüller?

*   *   *

One of the fascinating aspects of the study of espionage is that in no other
field is there such an intermingling of fact and fiction. I cannot promise in
every case to have successfully separated the one from the other, and this
one was perhaps even more difficult than most, but I have done my best. In
the larger sense I suppose it doesn't matter, since all these stories are
lessons and parables anyway. If they serve to illustrate some of the truths of
the game, then they have fulfilled their purpose. But I promise you that I
have tried.

PART FOUR:
TOOLS OF THE TRADE

If you've read this far, you've learned the rudiments, some odd facts and the lessons of the world's great spies. So what does a true spymaster have that you haven't got?

As Spymaster General of the FIB, there are some practical tools and gambits common among spies that should be in your bag of tricks. They're as essential as your agents or emmisaries. Following is a discussion of some of the basics.

Courtesy of CULVER PICTURES

16 THE MEINERTZHAGEN HAVERSACK GAMBIT

Sometimes in chess, or warfare, or baseball, or any other human endeavor, there is performed a maneuver that is so perfect of itself that it becomes a model for all future actions of the type. So it was in the field of deception in warfare with the Meinertzhagen Haversack Gambit.

The year was 1917. World War I was in full swing. British Colonel Richard Meinertzhagen was a staff officer for Intelligence under General Sir Edmund Allenby, commander in chief of the Imperial Army in the Sinai Desert. Facing the British forces on a line from Gaza on the coast to Beersheba in the desert, and holding up the British advance northwards to Jerusalem, was a combined force of the Turkish and German armies, commanded by a German, General Kress von Kressenstein.

Courtesy of CULVER PICTURES

Turkish patrol in advance of Gaza.

Meinertzhagen's problem was simple. Several previous British commanders had tried to break the Turco-German line at Gaza, and had failed. General Allenby had decided on a cavalry sweep around the Beersheba flank, which would be lightly defended as it looked like very rough terrain for cavalry.

But the defenses could be strengthened quickly, and would be if von Kressenstein saw any signs of a British build-up around Beersheba. But for Allenby's plans there would have to be a British build-up around Beersheba. So Colonel Meinertzhagen had to make it look like something else. What else?

A feint. Meinertzhagen decided to convince the German commander that Allenby was only *pretending* to attack at Beersheba to draw the Turco-German troops away, and that the main attack would come at Gaza as usual.

Colonel Meinertzhagen put together a staff officer's notebook, and crammed it full of the sort of stuff that staff officers would have in their notebooks—the sort of stuff that is supposed to be left in a rear area and not brought up to the front, the sort of stuff that every officer brings up anyway, feeling that, after all, *he* is invulnerable, that nothing can happen to *him*. He crammed it full of the date of the coming offensive, and the place of the offensive, and the troops to be used in the offensive—the date two weeks after the actual date, the place, Gaza (after a feint at Beersheba).

Now it certainly looked believable. How to get it into enemy hands in a way that they would believe? Meinertzhagen put the notebook in an army issue haversack with a couple of fabricated personal letters,[1] 20 pounds in notes, and a cipher key for the cipher then being used by the British transmitting station.[2] What German intelligence officer could resist such a haul?

On October 10, 1917, Meinertzhagen bloodied up the haversack with horses' blood, mounted his horse, and rode into deception history. He went north, in front of the British lines, looking for a Turkish patrol. He found one, and waited patiently for them to notice him. Then, with much excitement and signs of panic, he rode off. The Turkish patrol chased him, firing wildly in all directions. He dropped his rifle. They chased on. He dropped his field glasses, and then his water bottle. They closed in. He dropped the bloody haversack, and then escaped.

It must have been very artistic, and it fooled the Turkish patrol completely. Their description of the chase must have also fooled the German intelligence officers. They were at least half convinced.

Now for the finishing touches. From the British General Headquarters a ciphered message went out urging all patrols to be on the lookout for the lost haversack. The Germans, using the cipher in the haversack, read the message.

---

[1]   One of which, supposedly from a brother officer, confirmed the supposed date of the attack.

[2]   The aerial for which had been mounted atop the 450-foot-high Great Pyramid of Khufu at Giza.

Meinertzhagen had a message sent out demanding that he be court-martialed for losing the haversack. The Germans read the message.

Messages were sent which indicated that no British attack could take place before November 14, that General Allenby was going to be on leave until the 7th. The Germans read the messages. Messages were sent out verifying the place of the attack as Gaza. The Germans began moving some of their troops.

Meinertzhagen discovered that the enemy was extremely low on cigarettes. On October 29th, the Royal Flying Corps dropped over 100,000 packs of cigarettes to the Turkish troops at Beersheba—cigarettes that Meinertzhagen had had heavily doped with opium.

Courtesy of CULVER PICTURES

Turkish mounted infantry in action before Beer-sheba.

Allenby secretly moved his cavalry to Beersheba, leaving in their place 15,000 straw-and-canvas "horses" for the Turkish scouts to see.

At dawn on October 30, 1917, the British artillery barrage began, and the cavalry, 15,000-strong, attacked the city of Beersheba. The defenders were asleep; doped to their eyebrows with the opiated cigarettes that had so nicely fallen from the sky the day before. Within two weeks both Beersheba and Gaza had fallen, and Allenby was well on his way to Jerusalem.

And the Meinertzhagen Haversack Gambit had instantly entered the Spymasters' Hall of Fame.

Courtesy of CULVER PICTURES

General Allenby enters Jerusalem in December 1917—three months earlier and with much less loss of life than expected, thanks to Colonel Meinertzhagen.

17 DEAD DROP BY VICTOR SUVOROV

The author was an agent in the GRU, the Soviet Military Intelligence. Here he describes a part of his training.

Every free moment we have is given over to looking for dead drop sites. We poke about in corners. A spy needs hundreds of these sites, the sort of places where he can be absolutely sure of being alone and know that he had nobody on his heels, where he can hide secret papers and objects and be quite certain that no children from the street or chance passers-by will find them, that there's not going to be any building work going on and that there will be no rats or squirrels, no snow or water to damage what has been hidden. A spy has to have many such dead drops in reserve and must never use the same place more than once. The sites we need have to be away from prisons, railway stations, important military factories, and not in government or diplomatic districts, because in all those places there is heightened activity by the police and it is easy to be trapped. But where, in Moscow, can you find a place where there are no prisons or important government or military institutions?

We searched for these dead drops in all our spare time. We hunted for them in the woods on the outskirts of Moscow, in the parks, on patches of wasteland and in abandoned buildings. We searched in the snow and mud. We needed a lot of usable sites. And anyone who learns to find such places in Moscow can also do it in Khartoum, Melbourne, or Helsinki.

—from *Inside the Aquarium*

"*Perhaps we ought to advise headquarters that Agent Q-5 isn't the femme fatale she used to be.*"

Courtesy of the New York Public Library Collection.   Drawing by Peter Arno; © 1938, 1966 The New Yorker Magazine, Inc.

ANOTHER VIEW

When Bill had been in Cologne about a fortnight, Hambleton told him one morning that there was a little job on hand that night.

"There is a courier leaving Mainz Station at eight fifteen tonight for here," he said. "He has some papers in his little brown bag, and we are going to get them."

"How?"

"Goodness knows, it all depends on circumstances. I don't know anything about him, whether he's a big man or a little one, whether he'll have an escort or not—they don't as a rule, but these papers seem to be something special—whether he'll travel in a car with other people or in first-class in lonely majesty, or, as they say, what."

"Then you haven't got any plan?"

"Of course not, how could I have? Do get out of your head these ideas about elaborate plans which are so popular in fiction. You know: At eight forty-four and one half precisely you will walk past the automatic weighing-machine on the down platform, and a man in a pale-blue Homburg hat will pass you and murmur either 'Catfish,' 'Plaice,' or 'Cod,' or 'Salmon.' 'Catfish' means the courier is a large savage man armed to the teeth who never sleeps, with an escort of eight of the Prussian Guard so alert that they take it in turns to breathe. That's to let you know it's going to be a little difficult. 'Plaice' means that he will have a girl friend with him, so look out for squalls. That's rather a good one, pass the beer. 'Cod' means that, though he travels alone, he is a dangerous homicidal maniac who is quite sane till anybody touches his luggage, when a violent complex is suddenly released and he is possessed with a passion for peritoneotomy—"

"What's that?"

"What Jack the Ripper did. 'Salmon' means that he is a weak little man suffering from incipient sleeping-sickness. Salmon is never served up on our job. Even if you could remember all that, he wouldn't; your watch would be fast—his slow, so you'd never meet; and his pale-blue Homburg would be blown off his head at a corner and run over by a street car and the only other one he could buy would be a dark green one. Then we should naturally conclude that X 27 has been snootered and that this one was a counterfeit, whereupon it would be the stern duty of one of us to follow him out of the station and assassinate him without a sound or trace in a town you don't know, if possible without leaving so much as a body to mark the spot. The best way, of course, would be to push him under a street car at the exact spot where his blue Homburg was run over, leaving it to be inferred that grief at his loss had driven him to suicide. Pass the beer."

"But haven't you any ideas?" asked Bill.

"Oh yes, lots. We could merely hit him on the head with a blunt instrument, take his bag, and just walk away with such ineffable dignity that anyone who saw us do it wouldn't believe their eyes. Or we could crawl along the footboard in the middle of the night somewhere between Coblenz and Bonn, open a car door, which is sure to be locked, by pushing down a window which is certain to be securely shut, and once more produce the blunt instrument. After all, an automatic is a blunt instrument, isn't it? We may find ourselves doing that, it's quite possible. On the whole I think the best thing would be for you to sing to him, and perhaps he would give you the bag to go away."

—from *Drink to Yesterday*
by Manning Coles

18 INTELLIGENCE GATHERING: ONE EXAMPLE

What sort of intelligence do spies really gather? What sort of information does one country really want to know about another? And what conclusions can a counterespionage organization make if it discovers what it is that its enemy wants to know?

Half a century ago Germany[1] was at war with Great Britain.[2] The United States was not yet in the war when the Abwehr, the German Military Secret Service, ordered one of its agents, then in Great Britain, to cross the Atlantic and set up a new spy network in America. In August 1941, he arrived in the United States.

The agent, a young man from the Balkans named Dusko Popov, was actually a double agent, working for the British.[3] When his Abwehr contact in Lisbon gave him a microdot containing a list of objectives for his new

---

[1]   And Italy, and Austria, and Japan, and a few other countries.

[2]   And Poland and France and Belgium and Holland and China, and a few other countries.

[3]   He was a member of the very successful "Double Cross" system, under the control of the Twenty Committee of MI.5, the British counterintelligence service, where his code name was "Tricycle."

American network, the list was in the hands of Great Britain, and subsequently the United States, almost immediately. What did the Germans want to know, and what conclusions could be drawn from it?

And, perhaps even more interesting, what conclusions actually were drawn from it?

Here is a loosely-translated copy of the list on the microdot:[4]

> Naval Information: *Reports on enemy shipments (materiel, foodstuffs—combination of convoys, if possible with names of ships and speeds).*
>
> *Assembly of troops for oversea transport in U.S.A. and Canada. Strength—number of ships—ports of assembly—reports on ship building (naval and merchant ships)—wharves (dockyards)—state and private owned wharves—new works—list of ships under construction or ordered—times of building.*
>
> *Reports regarding U.S.A. strong points of all descriptions, especially in Florida[5]—organization of strong points for patrol boats and their depot ships—coastal defence—organization districts.*
>
> Hawaii:[6] *Ammunition dumps and mine depots.*
> 1. *Details about naval ammunition and mine depot on the Isle of Kushua[7] (Pearl Harbor). If possible sketch.*
> 2. *Naval ammunition depot Lualuelei.[8] Exact position? Is there a railway line (junction)?*
> 3. *The total ammunition reserve of the army is supposed to be in the rock of Alaimanu Crater.[9] Position?*
> 4. *Is the Punchbowl Crater (Honolulu) being used as an ammunition dump? If not, are there other military works?*
>
> Airfields:
> 1. *Lukefield Airfield[10]—Details (sketch if possible) regarding the situation of the hangars (number?), workshops, bomb depots, and gasoline depots. Are there underground gasoline*

---

[4]   In August 1941, the United States was still four months from being rudely pulled into World War II by the Japanese surprise attack on Pearl Harbor on December 7, 1941.

[5]   Why Florida? Perhaps because it juts out so far into the Caribbean Sea, and has to be gone around if one is sailing from Europe to Mexico. Through two world wars Germany remained convinced (Perhaps with some justification) that Mexico so hated the United States that she could be drawn into any war against her northern neighbor.

[6]   Why Hawaii? It is the piece of the United States that is furthest from, and of least interest to, Germany. They must have been doing their Japanese allies a favor.

[7]   They probably meant Kuahua, a small peninsula jutting into Pearl Harbor across from the Navy Yard, used for stores and supplies.

[8]   The Naval Arsenal was at Lualuelei.

[9]   Alaimanu is spelled correctly, and much of the ammunition reserve of the Army was in deep tunnels cut into the crater.

installations?—Exact position of the seaplane station? Occupation?

2. Naval Air Arm strong point Kanohe[11]—*Exact report regarding position, number of hangars, depots, and workshops (sketch). Occupation?*

3. Army airfields Wicham[12] Field and Wheeler Field.—*Exact position? Reports regarding number of hangars, depots and workshops. Underground installations? (Sketch.)*

4. Rodger's Airport[13]—*In case of war will this place be taken over by the army or the navy?*[14] *What preparations have been made? Number of hangars? Are there landing possibilities for seaplanes?*

5. Airport of the Pan American Airways—*Exact position? (If possible, sketch.) Is this airport possibly identical with Rodger's Airport or a part thereof?*[15] *(A wireless station of the Pan American Airways is on Mohapuu Peninsula.)*

Naval Strong Point Pearl Harbor:

1. *Exact details and sketch about the situation of the state wharf, of the pier installations, workshops, gasoline installations, situations of dry dock No. 1 and of the new dry dock which is being built.*

2. *Details about the submarine station (plan of situation). What land installations are in existence?*

3. *Where is the mine sweeper station? How far has the dredgework progressed at the entrance and in the east and southeast lock?*[16] *Depths of water?*

4. *Number of berths for ships?*

5. *Is there a floating dock in Pearl Harbor or is the transfer of such a dock intended?*

Special tasks: *Reports about torpedo protection nets newly introduced in the British and American navy. How far are they already in ex-*

---

[10] There was no Lukefield Airfield. Nor a Luke Field. The Marine Corps air base at Ewa was near West Loch.

[11] Kaneohe Naval Air Station is what they had in mind.

[12] Hickam?

[13] John Rodgers Airport, which is now Honolulu International Airport.

[14] The army took it over officially, but both army and navy made use of it during the war. All B-29's and other combat planes were staged through the port.

[15] It was located in Keehi Lagoon, halfway between John Rodgers Airport and Honolulu, but it wasn't opened until October 1941. Honolulu International Airport has expanded to include it.

[16] Actually they are lochs, "arms of the sea," rather than locks, "enclosed areas in canal or streams used for raising or lowering boats."

istence in the merchant and naval fleet? Use during voyage? Average speed reduction when in use. Details of construction and others.

1. *Urgently required are exact details about the strength of armor in American armored cars, especially of the types which have lately been delivered from the U.S.A. to the Middle East. Also all other reports on armored cars and the composition of tank formations are of great interest.*

2. *Required are the tables of organization (TO) of the American infantry divisions and their individual units (infantry regiments, artillery battalions, and so forth) as well as of the American armored divisions and their individual units (tank regiments, reconnaissance section, and so forth). These TO are lists showing strength which are published by the American War Department and are of a confidential nature.*

3. *How is the new light tank? Which type is going to be finally introduced? Weight? Armament? Armor?*

Expenditures:

1. *Position of British participations and credits in U.S.A. in June, 1940. What are England's payment obligations from orders since the coming into force of the Lend Lease Bill? What payments has England made to U.S.A. since the outbreak of war for goods supplied, for establishment of works, for the production of war material, and for the building of new or the enlargement of existing wharves?*

2. *Amount of state expenditure in the budget years 1939/40, 1940/41, 1941/42, 1942/43 altogether and in particular for the army and the rearmament.*[17]

3. *Financing of the armament program of the U.S.A. through taxes, loans, and tax credit coupons. Participation of the Refico*[18] *and the companies founded by it (Metal Reserve Corp., Rubber Reserve Corp., Defence Plant Corp., Defence Supplies Corp., Defence Housing Corp.) in the financing of the rearmament.*

4. *Increase of state*[19] *debt and possibilities to cover this debt.*

Air Rearmament:

All reports on American air rearmament are of greatest importance. The answers to the following questions are of special urgency:

I. *How large is—*

   (a) *the total monthly production of airplanes?*
   (b) *the monthly production of bombers?*
   (c) *" " " fighter planes?*
   (d) *" " " civil aircraft?*

II. *How many and which of these airplanes were supplied to the British Empire, that is to say—*

---

[17]   The Abwehr obviously didn't realize that, although most countries allocate money for years in advance, the U.S. Congress votes an appropriation bill every year, and changes every two years.

[18]   The Reconstruction Finance Corporation was established by Congress in 1932 as an anti-Depression measure.

(a) to Great Britain?
(b) to Canada?
(c) to Africa?
(d) to the Near East?
(e) to the Far East and Australia?
III.   *How many U.S.A. pilots finish their training monthly?*
IV.   *How many U.S.A. pilots are entering the R.A.F.?*

Reports on Canadian Air Force are of great value.

All information about the number and type (pattern) of combat aircraft. Quantity, numbers, and position of the squadrons are of great interest. Of special importance is to get details about the current air training plan in Canada, that is to say: place and capacity of individual schools and if possible also their numbers. According to reports every type of school (beginners—advanced—and observer school) is numbered, beginning with 1.

That's it.

A careful analysis of the document will reveal that it contains 902 words. Somehow this job always manages to involve counting *something.*

And, to further subdivide the count, the section on Hawaii is 307 words long. And the paragraph on Florida is 26 words long.

Some of the questions were originated in one place and some in another, and they were assembled quickly. The most obvious sign of this is the change in numbering systems from Arabic to Roman in different sections. We have the image of the Abwehr case officer running hurriedly about the German embassy in Lisbon, to the military attaché, to the political officer, to the naval attache, and saying "we've got this agent leaving for the United States. What do you want him to do?" And then passing the notes to the technical section, "Put all this on a microdot—*schnell!*"

Analyzing as we go along, we can conclude that, as a third of the microdot concerns Hawaii, *someone* is very interested in our Pacific territory[20]—almost certainly, as we've noted, the Japanese.[21] We'll get back to this.

The microdot instructions ask for a wide assortment of information. Some of it—the specs on the new light tank, the strength of armor in the new armored car, the torpedo protection nets, and the information on convoys "if possible with names of ships and speeds"—is the classic sort of intelligence that spies are asked to assemble.

But some of the data that this putative network of spies is being asked to gather is interesting for a different reason. The Abwehr asks for reports on shipbuilding (naval and merchant), dockyards, British payments under the

---

[19]   Read "Federal Government."

[20]   It wasn't a state until 14 years *after* the war.

[21]   If the Japanese supplied the questions, that would explain the idiosyncratic spelling of the Hawaiian names.

Lend-Lease Bill, federal expenditures "altogether and in particular for the army and the rearmament," and financing means and methods.

What makes these queries interesting is that they are the sort of questions that are usually answered by the military and naval attaches and the consular officials in the host country. And at this time, since Germany was still at peace with the United States, it still had an open embassy, and a staff that was quite capable of going over to the U.S. Government Printing Office and buying what it wanted out of that flood of documentation with which the United States government is constantly revealing itself to its citizens.

The implication for we analysts is that the Germans anticipate that their embassy will shortly no longer be able to gather this information. Why? Because it will be closed. Because Germany will be at war with the United States.

And why will Germany be at war with the United States? The Nazis are not noted for declaring war unless they have immediate territorial goals. And no American territory is at risk against Nazi Germany.

Will America declare war? Despite Lend-Lease, and America's obvious bias in favor of Great Britain, the American Congress is strongly isolationist, and violently against "foreign entanglements" and "fighting England's wars." And Roosevelt, whatever he may privately think, cannot declare war without the consent of Congress.

Why, it would take an invasion of American soil to drive the United States into the war.

Can Germany be anticipating an invasion of American soil? It certainly cannot be planning to do this itself; it has no access to American soil, barring the American embassies in Warsaw and Paris.[22]

And Japan is across 5,000 miles of Pacific Ocean from the shores of the United States.

Except of course for the Hawaiian Islands.

And one-third of the microdot is devoted to the Hawaiian Islands.

At this point we need to know how reliable the Abwehr considers this agent to be. We question MI.5. They tell us that Tricycle is one of their most trusted agents. And that as far as they can tell—and they have means of telling—the Germans also trust him.

So we can assume both that the microdot is legitimate, and that the Germans really want the information they ask for on it.

What conclusions can we draw?

1. It would seem that the Japanese have an intense interest in the defenses of Pearl Harbor.

---

22   And Budapest, and Prague, and Bucharest, and Sofia, and Belgrade, and Copenhagen, and Oslo, and Brussels, and The Hague, and . . .

23   Hoover somehow decided that Popov was the "playboy son of a millionaire."

24   Fifty-one fighters, 51 dive bombers, 40 torpedo planes, and 49 high-level bombers.

25   Forty fighters, 80 dive-bombers, and 50 bombers.

2. It would seem that Germany feels it probable that the United States will soon be drawn into the war.

Let me make clear at this point that no one source can ever be regarded as infallible and no one bit of information can ever be regarded as accurate. There are too many chances for error, misinterpretation, misunderstanding, and deceit, aside from the major risk that, whatever the enemy was planning, they may simply change their mind.

But there are some sources that are reliable enough and some bits of information that are important enough that you treat them very seriously.

And here we have such a combination. This document strongly suggests that the Japanese are planning to attack Pearl Harbor. And the source, vetted by MI.5, seems highly reliable. Our conclusion must be that the risk is real. Our action must be to have the military forces in the Hawaiian Islands in a ready status, and put them on full alert at the merest whisper of anything wrong. Perhaps put a picket line of destroyers and submarines around the islands, and keep up a steady patrol of flying boats.

What was actually done?

Life is far more complex than art. When Popov landed in the United States he was turned over to the FBI. But they decided not to go along with MI.5, and not to run a double agent in the United States. They didn't trust Popov. They didn't trust MI.5. Perhaps they were afraid it was all a trick to pull America into the war. Popov met briefly—he remembered it as being about half a minute—with J. Edgar Hoover, who told Popov that he didn't like his morals,[23] and that his information was "too precise, too complete to be believed." Popov went back to Britain, where he continued as a valued double agent for the British until the end of the war.

At quarter to eight local time on Sunday morning, the 7th of December, 1941, 191 planes[24] from the Imperial Japanese Pearl Harbor Strike Force began the attack on Pearl Harbor. An hour later a second wave of another 170 planes[25] swept in. By the time the attack was all over, two hours after it began, five American battleships and two destroyers were sunk;[26] three battleships, three cruisers,[27] and assorted smaller ships were severely damaged, the Army airfields had been severely bombed, and almost every aircraft on the island was destroyed or badly damaged. United States casualties were 2,403 killed,[28] 1,178 wounded. Were it not for the lucky fluke that the American aircraft carriers stationed at Pearl were out on maneuvers, American military power in the Pacific would have been effectively destroyed.

---

[26]   The battleships *Arizona* and *Oklahoma* and the destroyers *Cassin* and *Downes* were total losses. The battleships *West Virginia*, *California*, and *Nevada* were salvaged and refitted.

[27]   Battleships *Tennessee*, *Maryland*, and *Pennsylvania*, cruisers *Helena*, *Honolulu*, and *Raleigh*.

[28]   The battleship *Arizona* lost 1,103 officers and men when it exploded during the attack.

The Japanese lost 29 planes, and one full-sized and five midget submarines.

Courtesy of the New York Public Library Collection.

German spies training carrier pigeons for intelligence duty.

19 CODES, CIPHERS AND SECRET WRITING

*H*RMYARZRM FP MPY TRSF PYJRT QRPQAR'D ZSOA

—*DYOZDPM*

As spymaster general of Freedonia you are ultimately responsible for the safety and security of Freedonian codes and ciphers, and for the task of intercepting and breaking into the codes and ciphers of unfriendly—and not so unfriendly—countries. Both jobs are done by the FSIS, the Freedonian Signal Intelligence Service, but—believe me—you are ultimately responsible. When Sylvania publishes the exact text of your government's secret offer to Courlandt to exchange Freedonian peat for Courlandtian herring and two divisions to be named later, questions will be asked in the Freedonian ReichsRat. And it is *you* that the Rats will be questioning.

Because of the nature of warfare, and because of the pace of the modern world most messages, even the most important, must be sent by radio. And because of the nature of radio, it must be assumed that the message has been intercepted. Anyone with a tunable shortwave radio can hear any signal broadcast over these bands. There are tricks to hide the signal—disguising it as static, for instance, or on the sideband of another signal. But those who are not your friends also know these tricks.

There are ways to send long messages in an instant, so that unless someone is ready and listening at that precise moment, the signal will flash

▼ABCDEFGHIJKLMNOPQRSTUVWXYZ

by. But you must assume that someone *is* listening—and you will probably be right.

So the secrecy of Freedonia's communications rests on the security of her codes.

The attempt to keep messages secure, and the failure to do so, has figured in just about every war since the Peloponnesian. One of the earliest methods, as told by the historian Herodotus, involved shaving the head of a slave, inscribing the message on his now-bald pate, and allowing the hair to grow back before sending the slave off with the message. This had several obvious disadvantages. The message-bearing slave could not be dispatched until the scabs on his scalp had healed and his hair had grown in thick enough to hide the message. Since most important messages have a time value, this technique is of limited utility.

At around this time it occurred to someone that *intercepting* a message was not necessarily the same as *reading* a message. Thus even if your enemy captured your slave and shaved his head, it would do him no good if he couldn't interpret the tattoo.

There are two basic methods for safeguarding messages. The first is to disguise them so that they don't look like messages. Seemingly random patterns can be drawn on a wall or in the flyleaf or margins of a book that will be easily read by one in the know. There are a few such scattered about this book.[1] Secret messages can be written in invisible inks.[2] Secret meanings can be concealed in otherwise innocuous text, by agreed-upon definitions or special placing of certain words.

The latter involves using a grill, which is a piece of paper or cardboard with rectangles cut out, and the holes numbered. The grill is placed over the blank paper and the message written in the rectangles according to the numbers. Then the rest of the paper is filled in with an innocuous cover-message, incorporating the secret message, that will not raise the censor's curiosity. It is, however, very difficult to fit a normal-sounding message in between the rectangles.[3]

The former method, using agreed-upon definitions to send a seemingly normal message, is called an Allegorical Code. It can work well if you keep it simple. The longer and more complex the message that must be relayed, the more difficult it is to make a cover message sound completely natural. For example, let us assume that your agent in Vlad, the capital of Sylvania,

---

[1]　Copy the alphabet along the margin of this page including the bottom arrow. Turn to page 147, and read the message in the margin from left to right.

[2]　Lemon juice, milk, and urine all make acceptable secret inks in emergencies. The writing can be done with a dry fountain pen, or even a toothpick. To avoid leaving scratches on the paper, a cotton swab is even better, but the letters must be writ large. The message is developed by heat. This only works where the use of invisible ink will be completely unexpected, as heat is readily available to censors; most technical means of inspection, such as iodine fumes and ultraviolet light, will also reveal the message.

[3]　Copy the grill on the next page, cut out the rectangles, and read the secret message on page 104.

Courtesy of Walt Kelly Estate, Selby Kelly, Executor

has heard from his contact in the War Ministry that the Third Motorized Laundry Division has been secretly moved up to Shcheem, on the border with Freedonia. Why do they expect to dirty so many uniforms?

Your agent sends a letter to his sister Varya, in Graustark. Here is an excerpt from his allegorical code chart:

Apple Tarts	=	Infantry
Cinnamon	=	Graustark
Doctor	=	Secret Police
Duck Soup	=	Sylvania
Fine Brandy	=	Freedonia
Ill	=	Out of Touch
Little Children	=	Parliament
Peach Melba	=	Artillery
Pepper	=	Shcheem
Recovered/Recovering	=	Now Located At
Roast Goose	=	Motorized Laundry Division
Salt	=	Vlad
Sausage	=	Tank Division
Sick	=	Under Suspicion
Uncle Bobka	=	The Foreign Minister
Uncle Vanya	=	The Minister of State
Uncle Ziska	=	The Minister of War

Your agent in Vlad stares at this list. He picks out the elements he needs and ponders. He must produce a letter that seems completely normal. And so he writes:

Vlad, July 19

Dearest Sister Varya,

I have it from a close friend of Uncle Ziska that our dear uncle has gorged himself on roast goose, and the third one did him in. After a bout of illness, he has recovered by eating pepper. Nobody knows why this should be, but our dear Uncle has always been very strange.

Have you been to see our mother recently? I hear . . .

And, if the censors of the Sylvanian Secret Police see nothing strange in this epistle, the message goes through.

The great defense of the censors against allegorical codes, or any sort of code that is supposed to pass scrutiny, is the paraphrase. A story is told of a New York censor who examined a telegraph message to South America during World War II. "Uncle William deceased," the message read.

The censor passed the message, but changed "deceased" to "dead." The next day a reply cablegram came up from South America to the sender. "Is Uncle William deceased or dead? Please advise." the reply asked. The FBI paid a visit to the sender, bringing the reply telegram with them. They wanted to ask much the same question.

The second method of safeguarding messages is to twist them about so that, even if they are intercepted, they cannot be read. Of course, the proper recipient must have an untwister.

The general name for a method of changing messages into some other form is **code**. This all-embracing term includes systems that are not intended for concealment—morse code, for example, which is merely a means of transmitting the letters of the alphabet by means of an off-on signal. Morse code can be whistled, hummed, sent over wire, or sent as an unmodulated radio wave. There are also business telegrapher's codes, which are not meant to conceal, but to abbreviate. GOWER, for example, might mean, "have concluded deal favorably."

The two major forms of message alteration are dictionary codes (or book codes), and ciphers. A dictionary code is a system where one word or group of letters is substituted for another word. Usually the code words are unpronounceable five-letter groups. To make the task of decoding more difficult, common words will have several synonyms. The code book containing such a code will necessarily be large and thick, since all words in all usual variants, not just words of obvious military or diplomatic application, must be capable of being encoded. A column from the encoding side of such a book might look like this:

PARTY	=	RTPVW
PASHA	=	EPBOT
PASS	=	QPBYT
PASSABLE	=	VTYLX
PASSAGE	=	ERPOT, WOBHT
PASSING	=	ROPBE
PASSION	=	NJUIZ
PASSIVE	=	ZPONT
PASSPORT	=	TPLBR, JIQPM, XDEPU
PASSWORD	=	TMPQW
PAST	=	MPGRC
PASTE	=	RQPON

Whereas the decoding side might look like this:

JGWTV	=	INSIDE
JHXAA	=	MILITARY COURT
JHXTY	=	SLEEP
JIAPE	=	SCANDAL
JIBOQ	=	TANK CORPS
JICCM	=	FRONTIER
JIDRT	=	HAIRPIECE
JIQPM	=	PASSPORT
JJTNW	=	BROWN
JKBWP	=	GARBLE, GARBLED
JKJUT	=	FIELD GLASS

Sometimes numbers are used instead of letters in the code groups. One sort of book code that uses numbers takes its words from any available book instead of a specially prepared code book. Of course it should be a book that contains all the words that the user might need to make up his messages. The advantage of this system for spies is that a perfectly innocuous book that is found everywhere, such as a pocket dictionary, or a popular paperback novel, may be used.

The method is simple: The message is, as is usual, divided into five-number code groups. In each group, the first two numbers represent the page, and the last three, the position of the word on that page. If the book is divided into two columns, then the first two numbers represent the page, the middle one the column, and the last two the position of the word. This would be startlingly obvious to the cryptanalyst if the middle number were always a one or a two, so the rule is an *even* number is the left column, and an *odd* number the right.

As you can see, this method is restricted to the first 99 pages of text and, in the two-column book, the first 99 words in each column. There are various means to extend this. For example, the code group 21212 can be

A rotary cipher device of the Civil War period.

Courtesy of CULVER PICTURES

Courtesy of the New York Public Library Collection.

An Underwood cipher machine of the 1930s. Note the cipher wheels.

used to mean that, in the next group, counting starts at page 100. Book codes of this sort are surprisingly secure, as long as your opponent cannot guess the book.

A cipher on the other hand works with the individual letters of the message instead of the words. These can be altered in two basic ways: **transposition cipher**, which mixes the letters up, and **substitution cipher**, which replaces each letter in the message with another letter.

A transposition cipher is created by putting down the message in one direction and taking it up in another direction. Let us say that you want to send the message, "Do not trust Chicolini, he is a foreign spy. Agent Eleven." Your system might be to eliminate the punctuation and write it down in a series of 5 x 5 boxes:

```
D O N O T     O R E I G

T R U S T     N S P Y A

C H I C O     G E N T E

L I N I H     L E V E N

E I S A F     Q W E R T
```

You fill in the remainder of the last box with "nulls", random letters to take up the space.

Tommy Hambledon turned the contents of the matchboxes out on the table. One of them had a strip of thin paper underneath the matches, and on it was written: "Apples unobtainable, am sending onions."

"Leave cancelled, am sending instructions,"read Hambledon.

"I thought we didn't use codes."

"We don't, if you mean the kind you sit up at night with a wet towel round your head to decipher with the help of columns of figures. We have experts who do that, if it's necessary, but we do occasionally replace one simple word with another. 'Leave' is 'apples' because you hope there'll be an Eve or two about, and 'instructions' are 'onions' because we hope they'll be more unpleasant to other people than to the recipient. 'Best quality fertile eggs for setting' would of course mean 'a supply of bombs is being forwarded per passenger train.'If I assassinated the Kaiser I should write:'Send no more umbrellas,' and they would know at once that the reign was over."

—Manning Coles,
Drink to Yesterday

The message, which was written across left-to-right in each box, is taken off from top to bottom and arranged in five-letter code groups:

DTCLE ORHII NUINS OSCIA TTOHF

ONGLQ RSEEW EPNVE IYTER GAENT

To further confuse matters, the top-to-bottom rows can be taken off in a pre-arranged order, say 3-1-4-5-2, which will make it harder to break into.[4]

In the substitution cipher, the letter which does the substituting doesn't have to be a letter in the English, or any other standard alphabet. One of the

---

4   But not much.

old standards, for example, is known as the Rosicrucian Cipher, or, in grammar schools, as "Pigpen." Its main utility is that it is easy to remember. Here is one form:

```
A│B│C    J*│K*│*L    \T/    \  X  /
─────    ────────     \ /    \ * /
D│E│F    M*│N*│*O    S X U   W*X*Y
─────    ────────     / \    / * \
G│H│I    P*│Q*│*R    /V \    / Z  \
```

The pigpen alphabet is the geometric shape containing the letter—with the dot, if the letter has a dot. For example, the pigpen message:

as anyone can plainly see, transliterates to:

ATTACK AT DAWN.

The hidden code has on occasion done its job well. During the English Civil War, when the Roundheads under Cromwell were unseating the monarchy (and eventually beheading the monarch), Sir John Trevanion was arrested for royalist sympathies and locked up at Colchester Castle to wait for his trial. Since his captors were busy beheading even more important people on even flimsier evidence, he had little hope of leaving Colchester Castle alive. At the last minute he was given this letter, after it had been carefully examined by his gaolers:

Worthie Sir John: —Hope, that is the beste comfort of the afflicted, cannot much, I fear me, help you now. That I would saye to you, is this only: if ever I may be able to requite that I do owe you, stand not upon asking me. 'Tis not much I can do: but what I can do, bee you verie sure I wille. I knowe that, if dethe comes, if ordinary men fear it, it frights not you, accounting it for a high honor, to have such a rewarde of your loyalty. Pray yet that you may be spared this soe bitter, cup. I fear not that you will grudge any sufferings; onlie if bie submission you can turn them away, 'tis the part of a wise man. Tell me, as if you can, to do for you any thinge that you wolde hve done. The general goes back on Wednesday. Restinge your servant to command.

R.T.

The letter advised Sir John to pray, and so pray he did. That evening he asked to be conducted to the chapel to make his devotions and meditate. The Roundheads, who firmly believed in the miraculous power of prayer, could hardly refuse. And that evening a miracle was indeed passed. When his gaolers went into the chapel to take him back to his cell—lo!—it was empty.

Sir John had read the subtext of his message—made up of the third letter after each of the liberally-scattered punctuation marks—and followed its implied advice: "Panel at east end of chapel slides."

The basic system for substitution ciphers is based on what is known as the Vigenère Tableau, which looks like this:

```
    A B C D E F G H I J K L M N O P Q R S T U V W X Y Z

A   a b c d e f g h i j k l m n o p q r s t u v w x y z
B   b c d e f g h i j k l m n o p q r s t u v w x y z a
C   c d e f g h i j k l m n o p q r s t u v w x y z a b
D   d e f g h i j k l m n o p q r s t u v w x y z a b c
E   e f g h i j k l m n o p q r s t u v w x y z a b c d
F   f g h i j k l m n o p q r s t u v w x y z a b c d e
G   g h i j k l m n o p q r s t u v w x y z a b c d e f
H   h i j k l m n o p q r s t u v w x y z a b c d e f g
I   i j k l m n o p q r s t u v w x y z a b c d e f g h
J   j k l m n o p q r s t u v w x y z a b c d e f g h i
K   k l m n o p q r s t u v w x y z a b c d e f g h i j
L   l m n o p q r s t u v w x y z a b c d e f g h i j k
M   m n o p q r s t u v w x y z a b c d e f g h i j k l
N   n o p q r s t u v w x y z a b c d e f g h i j k l m
O   o p q r s t u v w x y z a b c d e f g h i j k l m n
P   p q r s t u v w x y z a b c d e f g h i j k l m n o
Q   q r s t u v w x y z a b c d e f g h i j k l m n o p
R   r s t u v w x y z a b c d e f g h i j k l m n o p q
S   s t u v w x y z a b c d e f g h i j k l m n o p q r
T   t u v w x y z a b c d e f g h i j k l m n o p q r s
U   u v w x y z a b c d e f g h i j k l m n o p q r s t
V   v w x y z a b c d e f g h i j k l m n o p q r s t u
W   w x y z a b c d e f g h i j k l m n o p q r s t u v
X   x y z a b c d e f g h i j k l m n o p q r s t u v w
Y   y z a b c d e f g h i j k l m n o p q r s t u v w x
Z   z a b c d e f g h i j k l m n o p q r s t u v w x y
```

The idea is simple and easy to use: The alphabets reading one way are for the key word, and those running the other are for the message. Let us say that, for some reason, you wish to encipher the message "My name is Captain Spalding, the African explorer."

Your key word for today is Groucho. So you write down your message, and above it you write a continuous line of Grouchos:

gro\u2009u\u2009chogrouchogrouchogrouchogrouchogroucho

and below it, with a one-to-one correspondence, you write the message, now devoid of spacing, capitalization, and punctuation:

grouchogrouchogrouchogrouchogrouchogrouch
mynameiscaptainspaldingtheafricanexplorer

Very good. Now for the encoding. The first letter you get by going down the "g" column to the letter "m". Now look to the left, and you'll see that the code letter is (curiously enough) "g". That's ok. Now for the next letter you go down the "r" column to the letter "y", and look to the left. The code letter is "h". And so on. You will end up with:

grouchogrouchogrouchogrouchogrouchogrouch
mynameiscaptainspaldingtheafricanexplorer
GHZGKXUMLMVRTUHBBGJWUHPFNCTRLROGLXJJUAXCK

Now you divide it up into the customary five-letter code groups, and your enciphered message looks like this:

GHZGK XUMLM VRTUH BBGJW UHPFN CTRLR OGLXJ JUAXC KJRGQ[5]

The only thing the person receiving your message needs to know is what a Vigenère Tableau looks like, and "Groucho," your key word for the day. He doesn't have to carry around any incriminating code books or cipher tables, but can write the tableau on a yellow pad when needed, and then burn the sheet.

A simple and elegant method of encryption was invented by Charles Wheatstone, an Englishman, in the 1850s.[6] It took on the name of his good friend, Baron Playfair, who demonstrated it at parties. The British used it as a field cipher during World War I, and it is still a sturdy and usable cipher if the people whom you are hiding your messages from aren't too terribly cryptographically sophisticated. In its simplest form the Playfair cipher works like this:

A five-by-five square is constructed with the alphabet, first inserting the key word (casting out any duplicate letters, like the second "o" in "Groucho") and then the rest of the alphabet:[7]

---

[5]   The last four letters are nulls, to fill out the group.

[6]   He also invented the Wheatstone Bridge, a method for the simple and accurate measurement of electrical resistance, which is still in use.

```
G R O U C
H A B D E
F I K L M
N P Q S T
V W X Y Z
```

Then the message is broken into two letter groups:

my na me is ca pt ai ns pa ld in gt he af ri ca ne xp lo re rx

Then the encryption is taken off by the following rules:

1. If the two letters are on the same line, the encryption is made with the letter to the right of each, except that if one of them is the rightmost letter, then you swing around and the first letter on the left is used (if you are encrypting the letters FL in the above square, then the letters IM would be the encryption).
2. If the two letters are in the same column, then the letter below each is used, except that if one is the bottom letter, then you swing up and the top letter is used (if you are encrypting the letters ET, then MZ would do it).
3. If the letters form a rectangle (the most usual case), then the letters on the opposite corners of the rectangle are used taking the one on the same line as the first letter first (the first two letters of our message, MY, are encrypted as LZ).

So now we take our message, and by referring to the Playfair square, encipher it as follows:

```
my na me is ca pt ai ns pa ld in gt he af ri ca ne xp lo re rx
LZ PH TM LP RE QN IP PT WI SL FP CN AH HI AP RE TH WQ KU CA OW
```

and then we take off the ciphered message, and transform it into five-letter groups:

LZPHT MLPRE QNIPP TWISL FPCNA HHIAP RETHW QKUCA OWWER[8]

---

[7]   The tradition is, in any five-by-five grid, since that makes 25, and there are 26 letters in the English alphabet, the letters I and J are treated as one. This seldom presents any difficulties.

[8]   As previously, nulls fill out the message

The same message is enciphered with the same key word, in two different systems, and the results are:

```
Vigenère: GHZGK XUMLM VRTUH BBGJW UHPFN CTRLR OGLXJ JUAXC KJRGQ
Playfair: LZPHT MLPRE QNIPP TWISL FPCNA HHIAP RETHW QKUCA OWWER
```

The Playfair takes a little practice, but once you have the hang of it, it is easy to use, provides good short-term security, and requires no equipment.

A FEW NOTES TOWARD DECRYPTION

In the argot of espionage to decode or decipher is to render a coded message that has been sent to you into plaintext. To decrypt, however, is to render a message that has been sent to *someone else* into plaintext. This is usually much harder as you probably do not have the key to someone else's message.[9]

There is a firm belief among decrypters that whatever one person has ravelled, another can unravel. This certainly was true until the age of the computer, with codebreakers from the Middle Ages onward showing an impressive ability to decrypt and read other people's concealed communications.

With the advent of the computer, codemakers now have the ability to generate immensely long and seemingly random chains of letters or numbers to use as keys. It is generally believed that high-level enciphered communications using these computer-generated keys are fully safe from penetration, and thus unreadable by anybody but the authorized recipient. But if this were entirely so, then few countries would spend so much money maintaining listening posts around the world to copy their neighbors' unbreakable messages.

The first task of the decrypter is to determine just what sort of cipher she[10] is dealing with. The basic test to tell substitution from transposition ciphers is letter frequency. Every language has a characteristic frequency with which each letter in the alphabet is used in a message of any length. In English, for example, the most frequent letter, E, has a far greater frequency than the runners-up, T, O, and A.[11]

A transposition cipher will not change the frequency of the letters, since an E remains an E, it just changes its position in the message. A substitution

---

[9]   If you do, then you are merely engaging in an act of sneaky decoding.

[10]   Mrs. Teasdale

[11]   The frequency of letters in English is usually given as E T A O N I R S H D L U C M P F Y W G B V J K Q X Z, with E occurring 13 percent in samples of random text, T 9 percent, A and O both around 8 percent, N 7 percent, and on down. Thus the first five letters, less than 20 percent of the alphabet, show a 45 percent occurrence.

cipher will change the order of the frequency, but not the existence of the frequency. For example, if you count up the letters in a sufficiently long cipher message and discover that the letter E has a frequency of about 13 percent, with T and O hovering at around 8 or 9 percent, you can conclude that the cipher is a transposition and that the language is probably English.

If, on the other hand, the letter J leads all the rest, coming in at about 13 percent, and several other letters cluster at between 7 and 10 percent, you can conclude that the cipher is a substitution, and that J is probably the cipher for E.

Beyond the simple substitution and transposition ciphers, the complications increase rapidly. Ciphers can be double and triple-transposition, and multiple-alphabet substitution, and any combination thereof. If your frequency count shows a flat distribution, all the letters hovering around 4 percent, then you are probably dealing with a multiple alphabet substitution—or a very strange language.

Although theoretical ciphers have been created that are incredibly complex, the complexity of ciphers in actual use is limited by the fact that the person who is supposed to receive the message has to be able to decipher it in a reasonable time, or the information may be useless to him. A multiple-alphabet substitution cipher that is transmitted by radio may be rendered unreadable if one of the letters is lost in the transmission. A triple-transposition cipher can become gibberish in the hands of a less-than-perfectly trained code clerk.

When creating your cipher-breaking department within the FSIS, hire people with a love of language and a love of puzzles. The sort of person who does acrostics while waiting for the bus would be good. Back them up with the sort of people who can't be dragged away from their computers to eat lunch, and you'll have the start of your own "Black Chamber."

For a good background in the history and practice of cryptography, I suggest *The Codebreakers*, by David Kahn. Try to get the hardcover, as the paperback leaves out several of the more interesting chapters.

For a good primer on the techniques of codebreaking, I recommend *Cryptanalysis*, a Dover paperback by Helen Fouché Gaines.

ONE FINAL NOTE

Good luck, spymaster general. The security of Freedonia is in your hands. Mind the basics, heed the lessons of history, and use your tools.

But remember . . . your principal tool is intelligence guided by experience.

GLOSSARY OF INTELLIGENCE TERMS

The Agency—An outsider term for the Central Intelligence Agency.

Agent—A spy.

Agent-in-Place—A spy who is already located where he or she will be used.

Agent of Influence—An agent who is used principally to influence the policy of the host country.

Agent Provocateur—An agent, usually of *counterintelligence*, or the police, who causes the organization he has infiltrated to act against its own interests.

Analysis—What is done to *raw data* to turn it into *product*.

AVB—Allami Vedelmi Batosag; the Hungarian secret service.

Base—Separate section subordinate to a *station*. Under the direction of a Chief of Base.

B-Dienst—Beobachtung-Dienst; World War II German cryptanalytic section charged with solving naval ciphers.

BfV—Bundesamt fur Verfassungsschutz; the Internal Security Office of the Federal Republic of Germany.

Black Propaganda—Propaganda that is completely disguised so that it appears to originate with the enemy. Could be a radio broadcast, leaflet, magazine, newspaper, or other publication. See also *white* and *gray propaganda*.

BND—Bundesnachrichtendienst; the Secret Service of the Federal Republic of Germany.

BOSS—Bureau of State Security (South Africa).

Case Officer—The one who controls an agent or operation for the intelligence agency.

The Center—The *KGB* expression for its own headquarters, in Moscow. By extension, the directors of the KGB.

Chief of Station—The person in charge of a *station*.

CIA—The Central Intelligence Agency. Known as *the agency* and *the company*.

Cipher—A regular method of concealing a message based upon its individual letters or numbers. Can be either a *substitution* or *transposition cipher*, or both.

Classified—Material that is determined to be sensitive, and is to be seen on a need-to-know basis by people who have received a *clearance*. The classifications in use in the United States at this time are Confidential, Secret, and Top Secret. May be further restricted by the use of a *code word*.

Clearance or *Security Clearance*—1. Authorization to handle and read information that is *classified*. The clearance level corresponds to the classification: Confidential, Secret, or Top Secret. 2. The process of investigation leading to such authorization.

Clear Text—A message that is not in code. A message before it has been encoded or after it has been decoded.

Code—A systematic method of transforming a text into an unreadable form so that it cannot be recovered by anyone who does not know the method. Specifically: such a method based upon entire words or phrases rather than letters or numbers as is a *cipher*.

Code Word—A word used on the cover sheet of a document restricting access to those who have appropriate *clearance*, and who have the need to know this specific information.

COMINT—*Communications Intelligence*.

Communications Intelligence—Information gathered by the interception of radio, telephone, or other messages; *COMINT*.

Communications Security—The safeguarding of radio traffic, and the techniques used to accomplish this; *COMSEC*.

The Company—What the CIA calls itself.

COMSEC—Communications Security.

Consumer—The end-user of intelligence.

Control—The *case officer* who is in charge of an *agent* or operation.

Counterintelligence—1. The protection of one's own country from foreign intelligence operations. 2. The protection of one's intelligence operations from penetration by the enemy.

Cover—A disguise with which a person or organization can hide its connection to an intelligence operation. Can be a real organization being used for the purpose or a *notional* organization created just for the purpose.

Covert—Clandestine; hidden or concealed behind or within something so as not to appear what it is. Said of an operation. Its antonym is *overt*.

Covert Intelligence—Intelligence gathered secretly.

Cryptanalyst—One who attempts to break into the codes and ciphers of another and recover the key (the specific method used to encode) and the message itself.

Cryptography—The study of codes and ciphers.

Cut-Out—A person or device that separates one agent from another agent, or from the *case officer*.

Dead Drop—A place where an agent leaves a message, or supplies for another agent. Can be a hollow tree, or behind the toilet in a public washroom, or any place that offers reasonable safety and privacy.

Defense Intelligence Agency—The intelligence agency of the United States Department of Defense; *DIA*.

Desk—The section in the home office of an intelligence agency devoted to a certain country or area of operations, e.g.: French Desk, East German Desk, etc. The *station* is controlled from the desk.

Desk Officer—The officer at home in charge of a country desk.

DGI—Direccion General de Inteligencia; Cuban intelligence service.

DIA—The Defense Intelligence Agency.

Diplomatic Intelligence—Intelligence gathered by, of interest to, or concerning a country's foreign service.

DS—Drzaven Sigurnost; Bulgarian State Security.

Economic Intelligence—Intelligence concerning the economic capability or planning in the target country.

Espionage—Spying.

Gray Propaganda—Halfway between *black* and *white propaganda*, it is propaganda where the source is not immediately evident.

GRU—Glavnoye Razvedyvatelnoye Upravleni; Soviet Military Intelligence.

HUMINT—Human Intelligence; intelligence gathered by, or principally about, human beings.

HVA—Hauptverwaltung fur Aufklarung; external intelligence service of the German Democratic Republic (East Germany).

Industrial Espionage—One private corporation spying on another.

Industrial Intelligence—Intelligence about the industrial output, and potential of a foreign country. Also intelligence about specific industries or companies.

Intelligence—Information gathered by research or by spying upon which decisions are based. See *covert* and *overt intelligence*; also *diplomatic, economic, industrial, military*, and *political*.

KGB—Komitet Gosudarstvennoy Bezopasnosti; Soviet Committee for State Security. The principal Soviet intelligence and counterintelligence organization.

Letter Box—A *cut-out*, usually human, that receives and passes on messages.

Letter Frequency—The ratio of the different letters of the alphabet to each other in written text; a ratio which varies from language to language. The letter frequency of an encrypted message can tell a *cryptanalyst* whether the text is a *substitution* or *transposition cipher*, and in some cases provide a strong indication of what language it is in.

Military Intelligence—Intelligence gathered by and for the military. See *strategic intelligence*, *operational intelligence*, and *tactical intelligence*.

Mobile Agent—One who is not stationed in one place, but moves about according to need. See *resident agent*.

Mole—An agent inserted into the intelligence or security service, or the diplomatic corps or military, who receives the most secret information and is in a position to mislead his assumed employers.

MVD—Ministerstvo Vnutrennikh Del; Soviet Ministry of Internal Security.

Notional—Unreal; nonexistent but made to seem as if there.

One-Time Pad—A cipher device; a pad with sheets of random numbers or letters, each sheet to be used once for encrypting a message and then disposed of. Decryption is accomplished by the only other identical pad at the other end. A very secure system if used properly.

Operational Intelligence—*Military intelligence* of interest to consumers at the level of corps and above.

OO—*Osobye Otdel*; Special Sections, Soviet Military Counterintelligence (1943-1946); came to be known as *SMERSH*.

Overt—Open or public. The opposite of *covert*.

Overt Intelligence—Intelligence gathered openly.

PHOTINT—Photographic Intelligence.

Policy Intelligence—Intelligence used by civilian policy planners at the top levels of government.

Political Intelligence—Intelligence concerning a foreign government or those in opposition to it.

Principal Agent or just "Principal"—An agent who serves as a *cut-out* between the *case officer* and other agents.

Product—The reports of an intelligence agency, after *analysis* has been applied to *raw data*.

Raw Data—The form in which information is collected.

Resident Agent—One who works from a fixed address or location. The converse of a *mobile agent*. Sometimes serving as the *principal agent*.

SB—Sluzba Bezpieczenstwa; the Polish intelligence service.

SDECE—Service de Documentation Exterieure et de Contre-Espionage; post-WWII French intelligence service.

SIGINT—Signal Intelligence.

SIS—Secret Intelligence Service; the British intelligence service, also known as MI.6.

SIS—Signal Intelligence Service; the United States Army's codebreaking section, from 1930 to 1947

Sleeper Agent—An agent planted in another country for some time, with instructions to do nothing beyond his *cover* until he is "activated" by his intelligence organization.

SMERSH—Smert ' shpionam (Death to Spies); Soviet military counterintelligence units. See *OO.*

SOE—Special Operations Executive; British service, founded in 1940, for handling secret operations in enemy-occupied territory. Disbanded after WWII.

Spook—Slang expression for a spy, a *case officer*, or any employee of an intelligence agency.

SSD—Staatssicherheitsdienst; East German counterintelligence service.

Station—The primary office of an intelligence operation in a target country. Headed by a *chief of station*. May control one or more *bases.*

STB—Statni Tajna Bezpecnost; Czechoslovakian intelligence service.

Strategic Intelligence—Intelligence of use to long-range planners, it can be either *military, economic,* or *political.*

Substitution Cipher—A cipher in which each letter in a message is altered in one-to-one accordance with an external letter chart or system of generating letters.

Tactical Intelligence—That part of *military intelligence* that is of use at the batallion level or below.

Target—The object of an operation.

Target Country—The country in which espionage operations are conducted, or against which such operations are aimed.

Traffic Analysis—The study of the flow of radio messages as separate from the contents of the messages.

Transposition Cipher—One in which the letters of the message are rearranged within the message according to a pre-arranged system.

Unwitting—Used unknowingly; opposite of *witting.*

White Propaganda—Propaganda which is openly from the country or organization utilizing it. See *gray* and *black propaganda.*

Witting—Knowing, knowingly cooperating.

Ze-2—Polish military intelligence.

BIBLIOGRAPHY

Here is a short list of books that might be of some interest to the Spymaster General of Freedonia:

Bamford, James, *The Puzzle Palace*. Boston: Houghton Mifflin, 1982.

Brown, Anthony Cave, *Bodyguard of Lies*. New York: Harper & Row, 1975.

Brown, Anthony Cave, *The Secret War Report of the OSS*. New York: Berkley, 1976.

Farago, Ladislas, *The Game of the Foxes*. New York: David McKay, 1971.

Farago, Ladislas, *War of Wits*. New York: Paperback Library, 1954.

Gehlen, General Reinhard, *The Service*. New York: World Publishing, 1972.

Kahn, David, *The Codebreakers*. New York: Macmillan, 1967.

Khokhlov, Nikolai, *In the Name of Conscience*. New York: David McKay, 1959.

Knightly, Phillip, *The Second Oldest Profession*. New York: Norton, 1986.

Laqueur, Walter, *A World of Secrets*. New York: Basic Books/20th Century Fund, 1985.

Masterman, J.C., *The Double-Cross System*. New York: Avon, 1972.

Montagu, Ewen, *The Man Who Never Was*. Philadelphia: Lippincott, 1954.

Pinto, Oreste, *Spy Catcher*. New York: Harper, 1952.

Read, Anthony & Fisher, David, *Operation Lucy*. New York: Coward, McCann, 1981.

Reilly, Sidney, *Britain's Master Spy*. New York: Dorset Press, 1985.

Rowan, Richard Wilmer, *The Story of Secret Service*. New York: Literary Guild, 1937.

Schellenberg, Walter, *Hitler's Secret Service*. New York: Pyramid, 1956.

Suvorov, Viktor, *Inside the Soviet Army*. New York: Berkley, 1983.

Tuchman, Barbara, *The Zimmerman Telegram*. New York: Viking, 1958.

Wise, David & Ross, Thomas B., *The Espionage Establishment*. New York: Random House, 1967.

INDEX